mary
kennedy

MERLIN
PUBLISHING

First published in 2007 by
Merlin Publishing
Newmarket Hall, St Luke's Avenue,
Cork Street, Dublin 8, Ireland
Tel: +353 1 4535866
Fax: +353 1 4535930
publishing@merlin.ie
www.merlinwolfhound.com

ISBN 978-1-903582-76-3

A CIP catalogue record for this book is available from the British
Library.

10 9 8 7 6 5 4 3 2 1

Cover image supplied courtesy of *TV Now* / photographer Beta
Bajgartova
Typeset by Artwerk Design
Cover Design by Graham Thew Design
Printed and bound WS Bookwell, Finland

Contents

In memory of my father, who died 30 years ago this year, and in celebration of his love of life and his wonderful sense of fun.

Foreword

In January this year, I was a guest on 'The Late Late Show'. I was nervous. I'd never been on the show before. I had been interviewed by Pat at the time I presented the Eurovision Song Contest in 1995 but that was in the days of 'Kenny Live'. Four years later I was in the audience when Gay Byrne presented his last 'Late Late'. This, however, was different. On January 19, 2007, I was on the set, in the armchair, being interviewed by Pat. That was a first for me. The interview had a broad canvas – "Life, love and the pursuit of happiness!"

During the course of the conversation, I mentioned that after my mother died, I came across a very old hardback copybook in which she had collected quotations that appealed to her. There are some beautiful pieces in the copy, some of them I knew; some I had never come across before and some moralistic ones she had quoted to her children as we were growing up. I never realised my mother collected these writings. The coincidence lies in the fact that I like to do the same thing, but not in a hardback copy and certainly not in the lovely handwriting and fountain pen ink that she used. When I read a book, however, I always take notes. I collect pieces of poetry that I like and sayings that I find meaningful. Like mother, like daughter, I suppose.

After the show, I had a call from Merlin Publishing wondering if I'd compile a book of quotations, from my mother's and my own copybooks. That's how *Lines I Love* came about. It's a collection of pieces from different sources and different periods of my life. They all have one thing in common – they mean something to me. Some are uplifting and motivational; others are of sentimental and nostalgic value and remind me of certain moments in life. W H Auden said of poetry:

৶

"A verbal art like poetry is reflective; it stops to think."

W H AUDEN

৶

The lines in this book make me stop and think – and reflect. They bring me comfort and nice memories. I hope you'll enjoy them.

Mam's Copybook

"Life, we've been long together.
Through pleasant and through cloudy weather:
'Tis hard to part when friends are dear
Perhaps twill cost a sigh, a tear.
So steal away, give little warning.
Choose your own time."

ANNA BARBAULD

ဢ

It's a very strange feeling to be reading through someone else's personal things. Someone who is no longer with us, was much loved and whose death has left a gap in the lives of her family and friends. It forces you to ask yourself some hard questions: Should I be opening these pages and reading anything I find? Would it be better to just throw it all away? Or should I consign it to the back of a bookshelf or the attic maybe? No I don't think so.

The hardback copybook, with yellowed, lined pages contains cuttings and thoughts my mother began to collect when she was a young woman. I discovered them in the chest of drawers in her bedroom after she died when we had the horrible task of clearing her house before selling it. Some are clippings from newspapers, sellotaped in position, others are

written in her lovely handwriting, with a fountain pen, like the extract at the beginning of this chapter from a poem called "Life" by Anna Barbauld.

My mother chose to write the whole of that poem into her copybook before she was married. She was young and healthy. And as I read it now after she has lived her life and died I look on it in a very personal way. It's a poignant reminder of those heart-breaking and lonely days when she died. I realise that if she chose to collect this piece it was because it was meaningful for her. This is what she believed. There's no fear of death here but an acceptance which is not surprising given my mother's deep faith and belief in life after death.

For me, it's a reminder of the reality of life; sometimes pleasant, sometimes cloudy. It's a reminder of the gift of friendship. But most of all it's a reminder that death is inevitable, outside of our control. It will happen. So we should make the most of our time on this earth, enjoy the good things in life, tackle the obstacles, cherish the friends and live life to the full.

These sentiments are clearly visible in another poem Mam included in her copybook. It's called "Had I But One Day" and it's a salutary reminder that we take so much for granted in life and that we should make the most of every minute we have on this earth.

ॐ

"Had I but one day of life remaining,
Then should I see this generous world I love,
The dawn, the noon, the glorious colour staining
The western sky, the stars serene above
With clearer eye than ever I employ…

ANON

ॐ

I should be much more eager to forgive
And sympathise, and help and love and pray,
Before the numbered hours had hurried past.
And that is what they must mean when they say,
Live every day as if it were the last".

ANON

ॐ

The contents of my mother's hardback copybook are full of sound wisdom and full of beauty. They're uplifting and offer insight into the kind of person she was in so far as these were the thoughts she liked to think. It's nice to read them again and to quote from some of them here. In a way it's like breathing new life into these thoughts, the ones that strike a chord with me.

One of the final entries is from St Stephen's Day 1945.

ઙ

"Don't be afraid to have ideals.
They are the like the stars.
We never reach them
But wise men plot life's course by them."

ANON

ઙ

 As it happens, this particular quote doesn't offer much new insight into my mother and her way of thinking. Neither I nor my brothers or sister were ever in any doubt that she was a woman of high ideals and high moral standards. And she took every opportunity to pass them onto her children. In fact I came across some of the maxims in her copybook that she used to pass on to me as I was growing up.

ઙ

"The appellation of "lady" should not be
given to a woman's circumstances but to
her behaviour in them."

ANON

ઙ

I was in no doubt about the message I was being given when I heard those words. There's a similar one with a similar tone that I happened on.

"It is with narrow souled people as with narrow necked bottles.
The less they have in them, the more noise they make in pouring it out."

ANON

૪

See what I mean. I was always amazed by her collection of sayings and often wondered where my mother found them. I don't know where she got them but I know now how she was able to quote them at the drop of a hat. She had them all collected together in her copybook.

If I came home with a juicy story or a bit of gossip, this is what she'd say:

"Two ears and but a single tongue
By nature's laws to man belong.
The lesson she would teach is clear
Repeat one half of what you hear."

ANON

૪

I suppose all of those lines are a reminder that it's good to have ideals, high standards, dreams and to reach for the stars. Sometimes, however, it's difficult to keep the chin up. Sometimes we feel we're rising above our station to have certain dreams, certain ambitions. Who do we think we are? The message in her entry from St Stephen's Day way back in 1945 is clear though. Why not have these ideals – if they're good enough for wise men…

It's far better to be living by that advice than to find ourselves in the situation described in this snippet from her collection.

❧

"He slept beneath the moon.
He basked beneath the sun.
He lived a life of going to do,
And died with nothing done!"

ANON

❧

One thing's for sure. That could never be said of my mother. She was a woman of energy, enthusiasm and optimism. There's a piece she collected which illustrates what she was like when it came to tasks and challenges. It's called "It Couldn't Be Done".

❧

"Somebody said it couldn't be done
But he with a chuckle replied,
That maybe it couldn't, but he would be one
Who wouldn't say so till he'd tried.
So he buckled right in with a trace of a grin
On his face: if he suffered, he hid it.
He started to sing as he tackled the thing
That couldn't be done, and he did it."

ANON

That's the sort of person Mam was. She loved painting and decorating and woodwork. She joined a class and by the end of it she'd made a bookcase and a piano stool, which she covered in velvet. She was always good with her hands, hard-working and down to earth. She wasn't one to be taken in by appearances either.

"Life is mostly froth and bubble,
Two things stand like stone.
Kindness in another's trouble
Courage in one's own."

ANON

Kindness was one of her defining features. She would never listen to gossip or innuendo and thought the best of everyone. There's a piece she chose to include in her book that I really like and which illustrates that personality trait. It's called "Narrow Hearts" by Jean Morton and it laments the fact that some hearts are so narrow that they have no time for fun or for friends.

"What a pity some hearts are so narrow
That they've so little room for a friend
So little room for the grace of life
And so little hope to lend.
So little understanding,
So little help to spare.
So little room for Life's tender things
In which every heart should share."

JEAN MORTON

ॐ

The first two stanzas are taken up with the tender things that a person with a closed or narrow heart is missing out on. And then comes the hope.

ॐ

"But even the narrowest heart we'll find
Will warm at somebody's touch.
So when in Life's walks we encounter
A heart that is cramped and sour
Let us leave just a smile and a prayer
And hope in the end they will flower."

JEAN MORTON

ॐ

She quite simply loved people – all people. She was kind, loyal and loved company and a good laugh. In fact there's a piece she included that is very telling. It's something Lord MacMillan said and Mam obviously found it meaningful.

ॐ

"One should take good care not to grow too wise for so great a pleasure of Life as laughter."

LORD MACMILLAN

ॐ

There are lots of other thoughts in this copybook that I find inspirational and motivational and I'll mention them through these pages. For the moment though, I'll leave you with the final entry, written in June 1977, after a gap of 31 years during which time Mam had got married, given up her job that she loved because of the marriage bar in the Civil Service, made a home and had four children. Understandably there wasn't much time for collecting sayings and poems in her copybook! The date of this final entry is significant. You see, my Dad died in March 1977. He had a heart attack one sunny Saturday morning during a golf outing from work. Mam was at home doing the normal Saturday things: unloading the shopping, getting the lunch and putting on a wash. And then the knock came to the door that turned her life on its head. I was the eldest, just finishing college, John, my brother, had just started working in the bank and Deirdre and Tony were two months away from their Leaving and Inter cert exams.

This is what she wrote.

છ

"God go with you in your sorrow,
Through the night and through the day.
May some blessing come tomorrow,
That will clear its clouds away."

ANON

છ

I cried when I read those lines. While I was heartbroken over the death of my beloved Dad, feeling that the world was a black, cold and lonely place and that I would never recover from those feelings, here was my mother, who had lost her husband, her support and her life partner. She had to carry on and take sole responsibility for her home and her family. Her pain, her grief and her fear must have been unbearable.

I had no understanding of that at the time but I do now and those lines she chose for her copybook, after so many years of no entries, say it all. I feel the grief, the heartache, the loneliness and the consolation that she sought in her faith and her love of God.

Accepting Death

"I know you're in a place where the sun shines, rivers flow,
One day I'll be there too but for now I have to
Stay a little longer
Be a little stronger,
See you in the place where the rivers flow."

TOM FOSTER

ॐ

These words always give me comfort and a sense of calm. They're part of a song and I can hear the melody clearly in my head. I suppose it's fairly obvious that the song is about death and the absence of a loved one which is always sad and lonely but there's great consolation in the fact that the person is gone to what seems to be a warm, comfortable, beautiful and peaceful place.

The song was written by my son Tom when my mother, his granny, died. He was just gone 15 at the time and he and his grandmother had an incredibly close relationship. They had the same gentle disposition and chatted for hours together.

They really enjoyed each other's company. When my mother died, Tom was heartbroken and between the time of her funeral and her month's mind he wrote this song and performed it at her Mass. I've always felt that the gentle disposition that he and my mother shared is evident in these lines: "the acceptance that the dead person has indeed gone to a better place and the willingness to be patient, knowing that they'll be together again in that place when life on this earth is ended".

That calm and gentle acceptance is also evident in another piece of music written at the time of my mother's death. My sister Deirdre is a singer-songwriter and wrote a beautiful piece of music during Mam's final weeks on this earth, while she was being cared for in Tallaght Hospital. Deirdre later performed the piece, to harp accompaniment, during Mam's funeral Mass. We also included a piece of her song on Mam's memory card.

ॐ

"Walk me to the water; hold me at the edge,
Gently release me to the breathless sky
Opening to take me as I soar.
Light me on my journey, echo words of love,
Light me on my journey to the other side."

DEIRDRE NÍ CHINNÉIDE

ॐ

That willingness to accept that the departed loved one is gone to a better place, the other side, where the sun shines and rivers flow, doesn't mean, however, that there aren't also feelings of utter devastation and despair at the loss of someone we hold dear in life. When my father died unexpectedly thirty years ago, while I was teaching English in France, I thought the world had ended. I didn't know how I was ever going to feel the same about life again. I had already come across W H Auden's poem "Stop All the Clocks" a few years earlier in college, the one that subsequently featured in the movie, *Four Weddings and a Funeral.*

ॐ

"Stop all the clocks, cut off the telephone,
Prevent the dog from barking with a juicy bone.
Silence the pianos and with muffled drum
Bring out the coffin, let the mourners come."

W H AUDEN

ॐ

I always liked that poem. For me, reading it as a 20 year old, it had love, loss, grief, tears and references to common everyday things that, even then, made it relevant in my eyes. It was when my father died though, that I understood it. From that horrific time on, "Stop All the Clocks" has epitomised the gut-wrenching horror of death and the moments when the bereaved feels, 'what's the point?' It's when you ask yourself, 'how can life possibly go on?'

※

※

 The night of my father's burial was cold and wet. It was the end of March. I sat in the kitchen at home in Clondalkin, late into the night, and hated the idea of him lying on his own in the dark of the graveyard. I wanted to take a fold-up chair and go out there to sit with him and keep him company. I will never forget the devastation and the grief I felt. There were no consoling thoughts of him having gone to a better place with sunshine and flowing rivers.

I stayed in the kitchen alone. Mam and the rest of the family had gone to bed. God knows what desolation they were feeling as well.

※

※

The words of the eighteenth century French writer and political propagandist Madame de Staël were certainly true in my case. My grandmother had died ten years beforehand and, certainly, I was sad. She was a great woman, 102 years of age. We looked forward to her visits to Clondalkin every Thursday. All children hate to see their parents upset and I felt sorry for my mother and thought I understood what she was going through but I hadn't a clue. I had been to lots of other funerals before my Dad died and sympathised with friends and neighbours but it's when death hits you in the eye, when somebody is taken from your immediate family, somebody with whom you've shared everything, that's when you understand death.

The funny thing is my Dad left this world in a way that was good for him. He was playing golf on a bright cold Saturday morning in March, with his work colleagues. It was a staff outing. As they made their way around the course, he would have enjoyed the game and the banter equally. He was a gregarious, outgoing, friendly and funny man. And then he had a heart attack. My Dad was too young to die of course and it was too sudden. My mother had to take over a young family on her own. But it was a nice way to go, playing golf. He would have made a very bad patient had he been ill later in life. He hated to be "sty-meed" as he used to say, prevented from doing things. In fact he used to always joke that there was to be no black and no mourning at his funeral. There was plenty of both. He would have endorsed wholeheartedly the sentiments in these lovely lines by the British poet David Harkins.

౭

"You can shed tears that she is gone,
or you can smile because she has lived…

౭

You can cry and close your mind,
be empty and turn your back.
Or you can do what she'd want:
smile, open your eyes, love and go on."

DAVID HARKINS

౭

And in the fullness of time, that's what happens. We smile, open our eyes, love and go on because the human spirit is resilient. It can hold sadness for a departed loved one in a special place in the heart. The lonely days, in time, give way to moments of lovely memories. Just as well really because the one sure thing about life is the inevitability of death.

Charlotte Perkins Gilman, the nineteenth century American poet and writer and a grand-niece of another favourite writer of mine Harriet Beecher Stowe, didn't put a tooth in it, telling it like it is:

"Death? Why this fuss about death. Use your imagination, try to visualise a world without death!... Death is an essential condition of life, not an evil."

CHARLOTTE PERKINS GILMAN

ॐ

I think that's so true. Until death enters our lives we concentrate on living. Death makes us remember that we only get one swing on this merry-go-round called life. We should enjoy it and make the most of the opportunities offered to us, so that at the end of life we can leave this world fulfilled and satisfied. That means making the most of the opportunities now and not forgetting that life is precious.

Remember the words of the Hollywood star James Dean, who died in a car crash in 1955 at the age of 24.

ॐ

"Dream as if you'll live forever,
Live as if you'll die tomorrow."

JAMES DEAN

ॐ

The thought was not a new or revolutionary one. Euripides the Greek tragedian from the 5th century BC felt the same way.

"No one can confidently say that he will still be alive tomorrow."

EURIPIDES

The message is crystal clear. I know that part of the reason I felt that horrible black sadness when my Dad died was because it was unexpected and untimely. I felt short-changed. It was a different story when my mother died six years ago at the age of 83. I did still feel cheated. After all, her mother lived to be 102. But Mam had lived a very full life always – lots of happy times, lots of sad times and lots of activities. She made the most of every opportunity. I remember when we were growing up she couldn't abide any of her children telling her they were bored. She'd always reply: "Bored? I have never been bored in my life." That was the end of that conversation because if it continued she'd find a little job for whoever was complaining – to relieve their boredom, don't you know. She was a great advocate of the advice given by Pope Paul VI, who died in 1978. He was elected pontiff in 1962 so he was Head of the Catholic Church during the years that she and my father were rearing their young family.

ॐ

I don't know if Mam was aware of those words from
Paul VI. She didn't need to be told anyway. She loved
life and embraced it with enthusiasm and energy. I
remember once watching the American sitcom
Frasier with her and "Roz" declared to the lads:

"When I die, I want it to be on my 100th Birthday,
at my beach house on Maui, and I want my husband
to be so upset he has to drop out of college."

FROM FRASIER

ॐ

Mam laughed at that one. She didn't aspire to the
lifestyle but she related wholeheartedly to the
mentality of living life to the full. On the other hand
she had no fear of death. Mind you, it wasn't a topic
of conversation that was high on her list of priorities,
although she loved to talk and would chat for hours.

Winston Churchill raised the topic during his life time when he said:

"I'm ready to meet my Maker. Whether my Maker is prepared for the great ordeal of meeting me is another matter."

WINSTON CHURCHILL

ॐ

My mother was ready always to meet her maker and I don't think her maker would consider meeting her an ordeal. She had great faith always and believed that death is the beautiful moment of the soul. I don't know if she was familiar with Henry Wadsworth Longfellow's poem "A Psalm of Life" but she would certainly agree with its declaration of faith:

"Tell me not in mournful numbers,
Life is but an empty dream!
For the soul is dead that slumbers,
and things are not what they seem.

Life is real! Life is earnest!
And the grave is not the goal;
Dust thou art; to dust returnest,
Was not written of the soul."

HENRY WADSWORTH LONGFELLOW

ॐ

Come to think of it, there's a good chance Mam did know those lines. She loved poetry which I'm sure is why she started collecting lines she loved in that hardback copybook of hers. And there are several which exude faith in the after life.

ॐ

"Close my eyes as you would tenderly,
Mourn not my loss, you have loved me faithfully,
And when the cold grey dawn breaks silently
Hold up thy Cross and pray for me."

HENRY WADSWORTH LONGFELLOW

ॐ

I love those four lines for their tenderness, love, acceptance, faith and peace. They remind me of the time we had with my mother as she was dying. She was in hospital for the last seven weeks of her life and it was a great privilege to be there with her as she was departing this world and preparing to enter eternal life. In his book *Divine Beauty*, John O'Donohue talks about the deathbed as a special place "more an altar than a bed". He tells us that our attention should be focussed on the person embarking on this solitary journey from this life to the next.

ॐ

"We should not allow ourselves to settle for being
awkward and unsure around a deathbed. There is vital
and beautiful work to be done there. When you realise
that the dying person needs your words and presence, it
takes the focus off your limitation and frees you to
become a creative companion on that new journey.

JOHN O'DONOHUE

The seven weeks with my mother as she was dying were very sad, heart-rending at times. There were lots of tears shed and moments of raw grief. But it was a beautiful time also, filled with love, with music, with conversation, with prayer. John O'Donohue also had clear ideas about one of the most beautiful gifts we can give somebody as they depart this life, *"… the gift of helping someone to die with dignity, graciousness and serenity."*

 We were present for our mother certainly and she was dignified, gracious and serene. He describes a person as being beautiful near death. The body is worn but *"…the countenance is infused with radiance".*

It was a privilege to be there for Mam and with her in those final weeks. My father died suddenly and there was no time for goodbyes. I will always be grateful we could tell my mother how much she was loved and how much she'd be missed. Not everyone is afforded that gift.

❧

"The bitterest tears shed over graves are for words left unsaid and deeds left undone."

HARRIET BEECHER STOWE

❧

Mind you, those lines could also point us in the direction of throwing off our inhibitions and saying what's in our hearts as we go through life, not leaving it till the last minute or until it's too late. And as for the deeds left undone, there's a lovely poem written by a woman called Nadine Stair. At 85 years of age, she's looking back and realising she'd do things differently if she had to live her life over again. It's called "I Would Pick More Daisies".

ॐ

"I've been one of those persons who never goes anywhere without a thermometer, a hot-water bottle, a raincoat and a parachute.

NADINE STAIR

ॐ

I think it's safe to surmise that Nadine was a belt and braces kind of woman who left nothing to chance. How different would she be, given a second chance?

ॐ

"I would go to more dances, I would ride more merry-go-rounds, and I would pick more daisies."

NADINE STAIR

ॐ

It would be nice if we all could say these two lines at the end of our lives but instead of "I would go", we'd be saying "I did go".

"The Cloths of Heaven"

"But I being poor, have only my dreams;
I have spread my dreams under your feet;
Tread softly because you tread on my dreams."

No marks for guessing where those lines come from. This poem is just one example of the beautiful writings of W B Yeats. Like many of his poems, "He wishes for the Cloths of Heaven" is beautifully crafted, romantic and eloquent, from the very first line, *"Had I the heavens' embroidered cloths,"* through to the closing lines above.

I have a deep fondness for poetry and have my favourites but I don't think I could single out one that I prefer over all the others. I like "He wishes for the Cloths of Heaven" because it's gentle. It's got echoes of romantic love, vulnerability, hope, and dreams – all very appealing. And on top of all that it's beautifully written. When I read it I get a lovely sense of calm and an understanding of the human condition that sees all of us, from pauper to prince, strive for love. Sometimes we're successful; sometimes we're not. Quite apart from the thoughts it evokes though, I love the sounds and the flow of the words. I like to say it aloud and enjoy the vowels, the consonants and the rhythms.

Poetry has always been a part of my life. As a very young child I went to Speech and Drama classes. They weren't called that at the time though. I went to Capel Street every Saturday on the 51 bus, with two friends from Clondalkin, Barbara Ann and Mairéad. In later years we graduated to an Elocution class in Islandbridge. Our teacher was Miss Margaret Murphy. She was a civil servant who had a great love of poetry and drama and who taught classes in her spare time. When I look back on those years now, I realise that she imparted to us a huge store of wonderful literature, poetry, prose and drama. We didn't appreciate it then but thankfully that huge store was absorbed unconsciously. As adults, all three of us have a love of, and an enthusiasm for, literature that has endured. We also have a debt of gratitude to our parents for sending us to Miss Murphy and to her as a teacher, for her endless patience, as well as everything else!

It wasn't all Yeats and Shakespeare though. We had very humble beginnings. I remember one of the first poems I learned was about two elves.

25

ॐ

"Rufty and Tufty were two little elves,
Who lived in a hollow oak tree;
They did all the cooking and cleaning themselves,
And often asked friends in to tea."

ANON

ॐ

I still know that Rufty wore red and Tufty wore blue and they each had a hat with a feather!! Not only do I remember that poem but I can still see the room in which I learnt it and the actions that Miss Murphy encouraged during its recitation.

My mother often reminded me of my early forays into the world of the feiseanna when she would bring me, shaking like a leaf, to the Father Matthew Hall in Church Street. I would line up at the side of the stage until it was my turn to say my poem. She recalled one year sitting in the hall as 84 (she was adamant that was the number) ten-year-old girls, including yours truly, took to the stage to recite:

"Lean out of the window Golden Hair,
For I hear you singing a merry air."

JAMES JOYCE

Those were the opening lines of the poem for that year's Feis in that particular age group. I'm sure Mam was saying it in her sleep for weeks afterwards. To me it was simply "that year's poem". Little did I realise at the time, that it was one of the 34 love songs written by James Joyce and first published in 1907 in a collection called *Chamber Music*. I can still recite it backwards and appreciate now that I was introduced to that level of writing at such an early age. And that my mother was willing to take me to those feiseanna which were nerve wracking but great confidence builders.

In more recent times, I have spent many nail-biting sessions sitting in the audience as each of my four children took part in Speech and Drama feiseanna. I think now it's more nerve wracking for the parent than the child. There's less mind-boggling repetition these days though because there's a choice of poems. Gone are the days of 84 different interpretations of "Golden Hair" or her ilk!

From those early days, Barbara Ann, Mairéad and I were introduced to some lovely pieces. How lucky were we to be learning Shakespearean sonnets and being given a taste for the beauty of language, its sounds and rhythms? We didn't necessarily consider ourselves lucky at the time, mind you. Shakespearean sonnets are not easy to learn at the best of times and at our tender age of around 13 years the language was a bit of a challenge, to put it politely. A pain in the neck and boring was probably how we described it then. The first few lines were never a problem. They're the ones that are generally well known.

჻

"Shall I compare thee to a summer's day?
Thou art more lovely and more temperate:
Rough winds do shake the darling buds of May,
And summer's lease hath all too short a date..."

WILLIAM SHAKESPEARE

჻

That's fairly accessible language. Sure didn't it provide the title for the television series, *The Darling Buds of May*, that introduced us to Catherine Zeta Jones and launched her in the world of entertainment. A sonnet, however, has 14 lines and after the first four it gets very complicated and extremely hard to memorise. Try this for instance from that same sonnet 18.

჻

"And every fair from fair sometimes declines,
By chance or nature's changing course untrimm'd..."

WILLIAM SHAKESPEARE

There's no doubt I found it difficult to learn those sonnets. I hated the fact that they were a compulsory element of our Elocution exams. The richness and rhythm of the language, and the beauty of the sentiments expressed went right over my head. However, as I read them again, I revel in them. My absolute favourite is Sonnet 30. I love the way the words glide from one to the other and I love the sentiments. The poet is looking back on times past, opportunities wasted.

ॐ

"When to the sessions of sweet silent thought
I summon up remembrances of things past,
I sigh the lack of many a thing I sought,
And with old woes new wail my dear time's waste…"

WILLIAM SHAKESPEARE

ॐ

The sonnet then gives examples of the memories that cause him sadness, friends who have died and loves that were lost.

ॐ

"The sad account of fore-bemoaned moan…"

It finishes, however, with a lovely endorsement of the positive force of love and friendship.

"But if the while I think on thee, dear friend,
All losses are restored and sorrows end."

WILLIAM SHAKESPEARE

Wouldn't you love to be such a friend, that could lift the veil of sadness from a person who's caught in regret? There's a buoyant, upbeat, pleasant tone to those last two lines that I find very uplifting.

Such was Miss Murphy's love of language that she organised for us to record two poems for our parents as a Christmas present one year. It was all top secret. After weeks of practice we were brought to the Tommy Ellis recording studios in the city. We recorded James Clarence Mangan's epic poem "Dark Rosaleen" and Hilaire Belloc's "Tarantella". It was thrilling to be in a studio, with headphones on, giving sound checks and listening to people talking about the A side and the B side. It was like Hollywood for us. We were nervous as kittens and it took a long time to get it right. It was worth every scary moment though when we were handed the vinyl singles with our names on them. And when we handed the records over to our parents on Christmas

morning, complete with our faces on the sleeve –
we'd done a photo shoot in the meantime, don't you
know! – we were ten feet tall and they were proud as
punch. It was a present they'd never forget.

I have huge affection for those two poems ever since.
There's no doubt Miss Murphy had a great ear for
sound. The alliteration in these few lines from "Dark
Rosaleen" makes it easy to recite and helps the flow
of the lines. You can almost imagine the Spanish
ships sailing over the water, to come to the aid of
Ireland against the forces of the British Crown.

ॐ

"And Spanish ale shall give you hope,
My Dark Rosaleen!
My own Rosaleen!
Shall glad your heart, shall give you hope,
Shall give you health, and help, and hope,
My Dark Rosaleen."

JAMES CLARENCE MANGAN

ॐ

There were no ships sailing in "Tarantella". It's about
a man asking a woman a question.

ॐ

"Do you remember an Inn,
Miranda?
Do you remember an Inn?"

The atmosphere is heady with wine, music and dance. And my goodness but the words sing and dance along. We loved recording that poem.

ॐ

"And the hip! hop! hap!
Of the clap
Of the hands to the swirl and the twirl
Of the girl gone chancing,
Glancing,
Dancing,
Backing and advancing,
Snapping of the clapper to the spin
Out and in—
And the ting, tong, tang of the guitar!"

HILAIRE BELLOC

ॐ

Instead of just reading those lines on the page, do me a favour and say them aloud. I guarantee you'll feel the music and the dance as you speak. You'll probably end up dancing around the kitchen with this book in your hand!

While we're on the subject of that eloquent French poet who died in 1953, I think it's only fair to mention another of his pieces that is embedded in my psyche. It'called "The Python" and was published in a collection of Hilaire Belloc's poetry called "More Beasts for Worse Children". My brother, John, learnt

"The Python" as a child and it was his party piece at family gatherings. In fact, although John is obviously no longer a child, "The Python" is still his party piece. And we wouldn't have it any other way. There's a ritual and a familiarity to a performance at parties which we all maintain. I look forward to hearing old favourites from certain people, including hearing John say "The Python". He stands up straight, in front of the fireplace and puts on a mock posh English accent.

დ

"A python I should not advise,-
It needs a doctor for its eyes,
And has the measles yearly.
However, if you feel inclined
To get one (to improve your mind,
And not from fashion merely,)
Allow no music near its cage…"

HILAIRE BELLOC

დ

The poem continues with more advice as to the proper care of the python and it finishes up with the revelation that the poet had an aunt in Yucatan who had a pet python.

Sadly, however: (We all join in at this point)

"She died because she never knew
These simple little rules and few;-
The snake is living yet!"

HILAIRE BELLOC

ॐ

 It's good fun, a family tradition and it's great for John because as soon as he has "The Python" out of the way, he can sit back and relax for the rest of the evening. He knows he's off the hook!

It's funny how certain smells, sounds and songs can instantly evoke memories of certain circumstances. There are other poems that bring me back to Clondalkin with my family and our cousins growing up side-by-side.

ॐ

"Up the airy mountain
Down the rushy glen,
We daren't go a hunting
For fear of little men;
Wee folk, good folk,
Trooping all together;
Green jacket, red cap
And white owl's feather."

WILLIAM ALLINGHAM

Whenever I hear those lines from William Allingham's "The Fairies", I am transported back to Auntie Eilish and Uncle Tom's house which was next door to ours. I can picture the two families around the fire in the sitting room. I can see my cousin Brian standing there in his speckled round-necked jumper, with his lovely black hair and a mischievous twinkle in his eye. He was about eight years of age. The lines he delivered with much gusto described the diet of the intrepid fairies.

ॐ

"They live on crispy pancakes
Of yellow tide foam"

WILLIAM ALLINGHAM

ॐ

He was only short of licking his lips as he recited those lines. And where is Brian now? He's a grown man, married with two children – a highly respectable type with no more speckled jumpers! Now it's just specks of grey in his hair but he's still great fun and hasn't lost the twinkle.

Another great family favourite that I remember with affection is A A Milne's poem about Christopher Robin saying his prayers.

"Little boy kneels at the foot of the bed
Droops on his little hands, little gold head
Shh, whisper, who dares?
Christopher Robin is saying his prayers."

A A MILNE

ॐ

There's a warm glow around that memory for me. I reckon it's because of the references to Christopher Robin in his hooded robe, all nice and cosy after his bath.

ॐ

"God bless Mommy, I know that's right
And wasn't it fun in the bath tonight
The cold so cold and the hot so hot
God bless Daddy, I quite forgot."

A A MILNE

ॐ

It's lovely, warm and endearing. I remember, however, a note of confusion coming into the poem when there was a mention of Nanny.

ॐ

"If I open my eyes just a little bit more
I can see Nanny's dressing gown on the door
It's a beautiful blue but it hasn't a hood
God bless Nanny and make her good."

A A MILNE

The confusion for me centred on what poor Nanny had done wrong to merit a prayer for her improved behaviour. My mother offered the explanation that she was probably a bit strict with Christopher Robin because she was his nanny after all. The notion of a nanny was new to me as well, so it was a puzzling part of the poem. But my goodness I loved hearing it over and over and I used to say it to my children when they were tiny as well.

I began this chapter by saying that poetry has always been a part of my life. I have lovely memories of the occasions around the poems I've quoted above and that's why they're special to me. They are an important part of my childhood memories.

'Fields of Gold'

"Many years have passed since those summer days
Among the fields of barley.
See the children run as the sun goes down
Among the fields of gold."

STING

ॐ

 I found myself in a situation during the summer that was very new to me and for that reason very nerve wracking. It was during a Novena to Our Lady of Perpetual Succour in the parish church at Graiguecullen in Carlow. There was a different speaker each week who addressed the people in place of the priest's homily. On the final night it was my turn to talk.

I had been invited to talk about my trips to the developing world, Africa, Calcutta and Sri Lanka; about the people I met in those places and the impact they and their situations had on my life. To say I was extremely nervous is an understatement. I was rattling with nerves. I'm not normally that anxious – I think it was the fact that this was a church and I was talking from the altar to the people who had come for this Mass. Given that this was the also the last week of a Novena, they had already had talks from very interesting and accomplished people. Speakers such as Sister Stanislaus Kennedy, who founded Focus Ireland, John Lonergan, the Governor of Mountjoy Prison, and Liam Griffin, the former Wexford GAA manager. To break the ice, and to calm the nerves, I started off by talking about my family connections with the county and that helped me to get on a roll about my childhood memories. In the end the 20 minutes flashed by.

After the Mass somebody came up to me and said my reminiscences had made him think of Sting's song 'Fields of Gold'. I couldn't see the connection myself but I went home and took out my *Best of Sting* CD and listened again to the lyrics of that beautiful love song. The lines at the start of this chapter jumped out at me and made me realise that what we think of as ordinary everyday events can really be fields of gold.

I grew up in a three-bed semi in Clondalkin, on the outskirts of Dublin with my cousins living next door. One of the highlights of our childhood summers was when we were told "we're going to Carlow for the day next Sunday". This meant a day on a farm at Fenagh, out by the Fighting Cocks pub where our grandmother had been reared. We knew we'd get to hide in haystacks, to break (sorry, collect) eggs, to feed the hens, to worry the sheep, to pick cabbages and lettuces to bring back to Dublin. In a word we knew we'd be allowed to run amok.

I was the eldest of the seven cousins and in moments of sophistication would tie a rope around a hen's neck and bring her for a walk around the farmyard – none of their rough play for me. Mind you the poor hen could have died of fright after we left for all I know. Mick, Kate and Sean Esmonde seemed delighted to see us and indulged our enthusiasm for the freedom of the farm. When we finally piled into the two cars at the end of a perfect day, to drive back to Dublin, answering the Rosary which my mother and my aunt would be reciting from the front of the respective cars, it never crossed our young minds that the Esmondes probably collapsed in a heap of exhaustion to contemplate the following week tidying up after us.

They were lovely outings but I never thought of them as "fields of gold". Until this summer that is, when my mind was opened to a different perspective. I can now envisage Mick, Sean and Kate looking at us kids running around their farm and delighting in our collective innocence, energy, joy and laughter. Isn't it nice to be able to get a new perspective on an ordinary life episode that happened maybe 35 years ago? I'll never think of those trips to Carlow again without thinking of those lines from Sting's song. They're bathed now in a golden sunny light.

"Young girl get outta my mind,
My love for you is way outta line.
Better run, girl,
You're much too young, girl."
GARY PUCKETT AND THE UNION GAP

ॐ

Song lyrics can be so evocative and remind us of different images and memories at various stages in our lives. These lyrics are the chorus of a hit from the late '60s called 'Young Girl', by Gary Puckett and the Union Gap. It's what I was humming to myself in the back of the family car as we travelled to Geesala in County Mayo for the annual two weeks summer holiday.

When I hear those lines now I think of being squashed and of elbowing and being elbowed, as there were four of us in the back of a Triumph Herald! I remember us all being given a bag of sweets to keep us quiet for the interminable journey. There were no personal DVD players in those days and at regular intervals one of the younger ones would bravely ask: "Are we there yet?" I remember dying to be a teenager and thinking that the song was so romantic. Now when I think of it and the inappropriate nature of what's implied, with this man fancying a young girl, I realise that aspect of it went totally over my head. Those were innocent times. The true message of the song wouldn't go over the heads of today's youngsters.

Another song I remember with great affection from those early teenage years is the Harry Belafonte classic 'Island in the Sun'.

ॐ

"Oh island in the sun.
Willed to me by my father's hand.
All my days I will sing in praise
Of your forest, waters, your shining sand."

HARRY BELAFONTE

ॐ

 I loved the easy melody, the velvet tones of the singer's voice, not to mention his very handsome face! Above all though, I loved the sense of the exotic, of foreign parts, bathed in warm sunshine. I suppose the seeds were being sown for my fascination with far away places.

My brothers and my cousins were less romantic in their musical tastes. My cousins next door, all boys, had a record player and the lads would gather and belt out heavy metal sounds whenever they got the chance. They were in their element. I remember many occasions when we had to listen to the likes of Thunderclap Newman belting out what I thought were very unmelodic songs. What do you make of this for instance!

ॐ

"Lock up the streets and houses
Because there's something in the air.
We've got to get together sooner or later
Because the revolution's here, and you know it's right
And you know that it's right."

THUNDERCLAP NEWMAN

ॐ

Each to their own as they say and there's no accounting for taste!

It wasn't just noise and weird lyrics coming from that house though. My Uncle Tom's favourite song was 'Scarlet Ribbons (For Her Hair)' and I never tired of hearing him sing it. Sinead O'Connor recorded it in more recent times. You know the story.

ॐ

"I peeked in to say goodnight,
When I heard my child in Prayer.
She said, "And for me some scarlet ribbons,
Scarlet ribbons for my hair."

JACK SEGAL

The parent (in my mind it's the father), goes in search of scarlet ribbons but the shops are closed. He returns home with a heavy heart, not wanting his little girl's prayer to go unanswered. All is not lost however…

ॐ

"And just before the dawn was breaking,
I peeked in and on her bed,
In gay profusion lying there,
Lovely ribbons, scarlet ribbons.
Scarlet ribbons for her hair."

JACK SEGAL

ॐ

There's no explanation. The Dad says he will never know where they came from, even if he lives to be a hundred.

It's a sweet gentle magical song. My mother loved to hear Uncle Tom sing it. It was his party piece at family gatherings and in her last weeks, Uncle Tom, who was unwell himself, sang it for her in her room in Tallaght Hospital. He passed away the following May and my sister Deirdre, who is his goddaughter, sang it at his funeral Mass. It's lovely how one song can bring us right back to very different moments in our lives.

*"The prettiest girl
I ever saw
Was sippin' cider
Through a straw."*

ANON

ॐ

How about that for an innocent introduction to a song? It's so different from the message of 'Young Girl'. I love these lyrics because they remind me of sing-songs in our house when we were children. They happened at various times during the year, lots of them around Christmas and New Year. 'Sippin' Cider' was my Auntie Marie's party piece. She was my father's sister, a woman with a smile that would light up a room and with a wonderful sense of fun. She'd sing a line and we'd all repeat it after her, adults and children alike. When I remember those lyrics I'm brought right back to those happy days. Like I said, songs are incredibly evocative.

The story goes that the prettiest girl and the young man sipped cider together and went on to get married:

*"And now I've got
A mother-in-law
From sippin' cider
Through a straw!"*

ANON

We'd all cheer and squeal with laughter at the last verse, although we knew exactly what to expect.

ॐ

"The moral of
This little tale
Is to sip your cider
Through a pail!"

ANON

ॐ

Happy days!

One of my father's party pieces was 'Indian Love Call', a song made famous by Nelson Eddy and Jeanette MacDonald in the film *Rosemarie*. Now my mother was a huge fan of Nelson Eddy and I'm not sure she fully appreciated her husband's rendition of such a hauntingly beautiful and romantic number. These are my favourite lines from the song and when I think of them I can see my father standing between the sitting room and the dining room, with his left arm raised and resting on the door-jamb. I'm transported back to very gentle times, growing up in a secure family set-up with lots of people around.

ॐ

"…When you hear my love call ringing clear
And I hear your answering echo so dear.
Then I will know our love will become true.
You'll belong to me and I'll belong to you."

OSCAR HAMMERSTEIN/OTTO HARBARCH

Dad had another party piece, 'Frankie and Johnny', which expressed very different sentiments to the sincere and romantic love of the 'Indian Love Call'. He used to perform it with great gusto and, like his sister, Auntie Marie, singing 'Sippin' Cider', we all knew the words by heart and would join in for the punch line: "*he was her man but he's doin her wrong.*"

You see the story goes:

> "*Frankie and Johnny were lovers,*
> *Lordy oh how they did love.*
> *They swore to be true to each other,*
> *Just as true as the stars above.*
> (All join in now....)
> *He was her man but he's doin' her wrong.*"
>
> TRADITIONAL

ॐ

Anyway Frankie gave Johnny money to buy clothes and found him in a bar in the arms of Nellie Bligh! Like I said, he was her man but he was doing her wrong!

47

"And what happened next?" I hear you ask.

ॐ

"Frankie went home in a hurry,
She didn't go for fun.
She hurried home to get a hold of
A big forty-four gun.
(And again…)
He's her man but he's doin' her wrong."

TRADITIONAL

ॐ

Need I say more?

We loved that song. And I love remembering those parties and sing-songs and the simple fun we had growing up – before the days of press button entertainment.

The Growing Years

*"You can tell me anything and I will
listen and laugh
or listen and cry
or listen and do nothing at all
except love you-
indisputably,
irrefutably,
infinitum."*

JAYNE JAUDON FERRER

☙

I was delighted when I came across these lines in a collection of poetry called *Dancing with My Daughter* by an American writer Jayne Jaudon Ferrer because, in a far less poetic way, I've been giving my children the same message since they were very small. It's affirming to know that others have been doing the same thing.

No matter how many baby books and mothering manuals we read, parents realise that all bets are off when the children get that bit older. You have to accept that they have their own personalities, their own needs and their own pressures. That's when we hope they realise that they can tell us anything and we will be happy for them, sad for them, worried for them, but no matter what, we will always and in all ways love them.

A mother's instinct is to protect her children and to do her best for them always. The same is true of fathers and there's a lovely reference to that in one of the Irish novelist, Niall Williams' books, *Only Say the Word*.

❧

"I know the harrowing the world has
already made in the soft places of your
spirit. I know your fears and your pains
and because I am your father, I cannot
know them for an instant without
wanting to make them pass."

NIALL WILLIAMS

❧

The hardest thing for a parent is to let go because for so many years when our children are small we're in there beside them, holding them, doing everything for them, protecting them and always watching out for them.

Jayne Jaudon Ferrer has another book of poems called *A Mother of Sons* and there's a lovely piece in it called "Midnight Rendezvous" which brings me right back to the early baby days. Those first days which every mother of a new-born will have experienced…even the ones who have those wonder babies who, allegedly, sleep through the night from day one!

ॐ

"It is with something less than
maternal goodwill that I crawl,
asleep and annoyed,
from my coveted bed
to silence your angry screams
violating the night."

JAYNE JAUDON FERRER

ॐ

The encounter continues of course until the baby is settled and sleeping peacefully in mother's arms and the poem finishes:

"My last trace of irritation
over interrupted sleep
dissipates in a hug, a kiss, and a smile.
You will never remember
these midnight moments together;
I will never forget."

JAYNE JAUDON FERRER

And it's true. We never forget. As in this poem, we look back with nostalgia to those baby days but at the time we couldn't wait to see the back of them, as we yearned for a decent night's sleep. I often think it's such a pity that these beautiful bundles of joy come into our lives when we are at our lowest ebb, going around in a state of constant and utter exhaustion, recovering from a birth and suffering from sleep deprivation.

Oscar Wilde said: "It's a great pity that youth has been wasted on the young" and you could apply the same logic to babies coming into our lives when we are too tired to genuinely enjoy them. We dedicate our lives to them, nourish, teach and play with them. We give them every opportunity we can but we do tend to be looking to the future a lot – looking forward to when they can feed themselves, dress themselves, walk to school on their own…and then all of a sudden they're grown up and in some ways they're gone.

I find myself looking back at baby photos and realising that I had no notion of how quickly those years would pass – in a whisper. I'd love the opportunity to have some of those moments back again. I'd love if I could just sit and hold one of my babies' fingers without having to think about the next feed or other chores that had to be done…to just be and live in the moment.

While I was on holidays in France during the summer with my grown-up children, I spent time sitting by the pool observing mothers with babies and toddlers. To a woman, those Mums were attentive, vigilant even. They walked along behind their children for fear they'd fall, held them in the water and played with them. They gave them bottles and yogurts and soothed the children when they got tired and cranky. Their own lives were on hold. I remembered being that soldier.

Motherhood is a most precious gift. It's the best thing that's happened to me and I know I'm not unique in that. From the moment your first baby is born, your life is transformed. There are ways in which motherhood is pure delight.

ॐ

"All that I knew of heaven
I saw in my babies' eyes."

EMILY ORR

ॐ

Those lines are from a poem called "The Witless Mother" by Belfast poet Emily Orr. Let's face it, there are ways in which we become witless when we have a baby. I know I did. For a full six weeks after I had my first baby I felt totally overwhelmed, I was exhausted and tearful. There were days when I was still in my dressing-gown at tea time. I just hadn't had the time to get dressed. That's difficult to accept when you've been totally in control of your life up to that point. And because this is your first experience of motherhood, you don't know when this feeling of helplessness is going to end. You can't see the light at the end of the tunnel. There's no doubt that there are ways in which motherhood is difficult.

ॐ

"Lord, thou art hard on mothers:
We suffer in their coming and their going;
And tho' I grudge them not, I weary, weary
Of the long sorrow — And yet I have my joy:
My sons were faithful, and they fought."

PADRAIC PEARSE

ॐ

Now I'm not suggesting for a minute that Padraic Pearse's poem *The Mother* is a typical example of the challenges of modern motherhood. It was after all written in 1916, at the beginning of the last century. This mother was about to lose both her sons to execution. There are, however, depths of maternal feeling here that are universal: the weariness, the sorrow and the joy. Mothers worry all of the time: Is my child healthy and happy? Am I passing on the correct values? Are my children listening?

These words echo all mothers' concerns:

"Have I taught you the right things,
my darlings?
Between laundry and table-setting,
Ironing and pants-hemming,
Manners and morals and
Where to pin the corsage,
Did I remember to teach you about love?
About listening and hearing
And holding and helping."

JAYNE JAUDON FERRER

ॐ

There are times, as we travel along the path of motherhood, that we need reminding that we are very lucky and privileged to have given birth. No matter what worries or anguish we feel as mothers we must remember that. I came across a quote while I was at a post-natal low ebb years ago and I cut it out and kept it.

ॐ

"Think always, that having the child at your breast
And having it in your arms,
You have God's blessing there."

ELIZABETH CLINTON

It's a very simple thought. I know I didn't fully appreciate Elizabeth Clinton's message at the time. I simply used it as an encouragement to keep me going in those exhausting days. But I fully understand the truth of it now and I cherish the memory of those early baby days, sleepless nights and all, which pass so quickly by.

We all want the best for our children and we all want our children to be the best. I don't mean "best" in a competitive or academic way. We want them to be the best of people – people who are honest, fair, compassionate, loving, happy and healthy. The list of qualities is endless. As I was saying, when they get older we see their personalities develop and we have to accept that they are their own people. Listen to the words of Kahlil Gibran when The Prophet speaks of children.

ℛ

"You may give them your love but not your thoughts,
For they have their own thoughts.
You may house their bodies but not their souls,
For their souls dwell in the house of tomorrow, which
you cannot visit, not even in your dreams.
You may strive to be like them, but seek not to make
them like you.
For life goes not backward nor tarries with yesterday."
                                                KAHLIL GIBRAN

All of a sudden comes the moment when they start to spread their wings, to socialise with friends and to want to do things their way. Sometimes their way is not our way but we have to respect their individuality and desires.

The words of the nineteenth century American poet and philosopher Henry David Thoreau come to mind:

> *"If a man does not keep pace with his companions,*
> *Perhaps it's because he hears a different drummer.*
> *Let him step to the music he hears,*
> *However measured or far away."*
>
> HENRY DAVID THOREAU

ৰ

I love those lines. They're open, magnanimous, gracious and show an acceptance of difference and of alternative life styles. They are a salutary lesson in these days of the Celtic Tiger when so many people seem hell bent on making more money, on buying bigger cars and houses and on running themselves into the ground.

I suppose the lesson for mothers is that we have to let go, to allow our children to move on and away from us and be their own person, secure in the knowledge that we are always there for them, that we love them and that we know them intimately.

Patrick Kavanagh gives a lovely reminder of the innate knowledge a mother has of her child in his poem "In Memory of My Mother Died 10 November 1945".

ॐ

"You will have the road gate open, and the
front door ajar
The kettle boiling and a table set
By the window looking out at the sycamores…

You will know I am coming though I send no word
For you were lover who could tell
A man's thoughts – my thoughts – though I hid them
Through you I knew woman and did not fear
her spell."

PATRICK KAVANAGH

ॐ

There's nothing more sure than that a mother's instinct is very strong when it comes to the person she has carried in her womb for nine months and then cared for through baby, toddler, child, adolescent, teenage and young adult years.

We give our children unconditional love and support, with the wisdom and experience we have garnered in life. We hope, as in Patrick Kavanagh's case, that through us, our children will get a knowledge and an understanding of the world and its people. And as they grow up and move away, we will, like Kavanagh's mother, always have the gate open, the door ajar and the kettle on.

And we hope that as adults they will feel towards us the love and the warmth that another Irishman John O'Donohue displays for his mother Josie in his beautiful poem "Beannacht" (Blessing).

ॐ

"And when your eyes
freeze behind
the grey window
and the ghost of loss
gets in to you,
may a flock of colours,
indigo, red, green,
and azure blue
come to awaken in you
a meadow of delight.

JOHN O'DONOHUE

ॐ

What I like about those lines is the understanding on the part of the son that as time marches on and children become adults, parents feel a sense of loss. There's an inevitable sadness, a greyness and a loneliness involved in this process. He knows this and wishes for colour and delight to be a part of his mother's life at that time.

The poem finishes with a warm declaration of love and protection.

ॐ

"And so may a slow
wind work these words
of love around you,
an invisible cloak
to mind your life."
JOHN O'DONOHUE

ॐ

Wouldn't any mother be delighted, after all her years of rearing and caring, for her child to feel like that about her?

"Seeing Through Different Eyes"

"A horizonless frying pan of desolation,
A sundried moonscape of cracked earth harder
than iron,
Grotesque lava heaps rising to the heights of ten
storey buildings,
Vast plains of dehydrated thorn scrub,
Siteless deserts and scorched black mountains."

CHARLES MILLAR

❧

The place described here doesn't sound particularly inviting now does it? You wouldn't exactly be chomping at the bit to jump on a plane and visit. The quote refers to the Turkana Desert in the extreme north of Kenya, not far from the Sudanese border. As it happens I was there just after Easter and I'm so glad I hadn't come across this description before I travelled. If I had, instead of wonderful excitement and anticipation at visiting a new place, I would have been filled with trepidation and a feeling of dread at the thought of having to spend time in this "frying pan of desolation".

The journey north took longer than I had anticipated. After a two hour flight from Nairobi to Lokichoggio Airstrip, in a small plane, there followed a three hour drive in a pick-up truck, over sand and rocks, to get us to Turkwell, a tiny village with 5,000 people in the province of Lodwar. The journey brought me into the Kakuma Refugee Camp run by the United Nations which is home to about 70,000 displaced people, mostly Sudanese. These people live in dreadfully cramped and impoverished conditions. And yet I don't think the words "desolation" and "grotesque" capture the reality of the Turkana – the place or the people. Hopefully I can show a different scenario to that described by the writer, Charles Millar.

Yes it's hot. Yes it's dry. Yes it's arid. But it's also home to half a million wonderful people, members of the Turkana tribe who are tall, thin, proud and hard-working. They are a mixture of nomadic people, who live a traditional life moving with their livestock in search of vegetation and water, and settled people, who have lost their animals in cattle raids from other tribes. The tribe's attire is colourful as they wear rows and rows of brightly coloured beads around their necks, long check cloaks and beaded belts. The

Turkana culture is an old and rich one, full of tradition. The songs and dances they perform to welcome visitors to their community are intricate, and have been passed down intact, from generation to generation.

If you saw the movie *The Constant Gardener* with Ralph Fiennes you'll have had a glimpse of how the Turkana live as part of the film was shot in their region. It featured the tiny airport at Lokichoggio, the beautiful Lake Turkana and the cattle-raiding parties from Sudan, who make regular forays into Turkana camps, making the tribe's life that bit more difficult. There's no doubt that they have hard lives. They struggle to eke out a living, in very harsh physical circumstances but they are a spiritual, caring, strong and joyous people.

ॐ

"Africa is a cruel country; it takes your heart and grinds it into powdered stone — and no one minds."

ELSPETH HUXLEY

ॐ

The thoughts above from the writer Elspeth Huxley's autobiography of an African childhood, *The Flame Trees of Thika,* remind me of how I felt after leaving the Turkana.

"May you see what you see through different eyes,
May you hear with different ears,
May you taste what you have never tasted
And go further than yourself."

A MAASAI SAYING

ॐ

For me, this Maasai saying sums up the need to be open and positive, without prejudice and preconceived assumptions.

The Maasai are another proud Kenyan tribe. Their style is different to that of the Turkana, as they arrange the beads differently around their necks, but it is equally bright and colourful. They also have a rich culture. By our standards in the developed western world, the Maasai live a primitive life, without essentials such as running water, electricity and domestic appliances. Their lives are a struggle against poverty, hunger, drought, and disease. But we would be well advised to embrace the wisdom of the Maasai saying.

I travelled in the back of a jeep with a Maasai warrior last Easter. As we drove along he pointed out many things, including yellow berries whose juice was enough to cure snake bites. As a young Maasai, he had become a warrior at the age of 16 when, as part of his initiation, he went out hunting in the bush with the elders of his tribe. After a few hours, they encircled a lion and he was the one to make the kill. This made him a warrior and a hero in his community. In some ways it's like the GAA heroes we revere in our country. People like Eddie Keher, Christy Ring, the Bomber Liston. They may not have killed any lions but they saw off the enemy none the less!

That Maasai saying always reminds me that it's so important to see things from the other person's perspective. The people of Africa need us to throw off our western standards and values when we meet them. They need us to see them with "different eyes" and to recognise that they are a proud and dignified people who have suffered injustice, who sometimes live in volatile political and economic situations and who have been forced to endure drought, hunger and disease. They need our help and we should feel morally bound to look out for our fellow man.

ॐ

"Unless there is room in our reality to embrace and touch
the lives of those who have no chance without us,
Unless we reach out our hands from our world
and touch the lives of those
whose worlds we cannot begin to comprehend,
We deny something essential in ourselves."

MICHAEL MEEGAN

Michael Meegan is an Irish man who has spent 28 years working for, and with, the people of Africa. His book *All Will Be Well* chronicles some of his experiences during that time and his conviction that the people of Africa deserve our help and support. He believes that by showing love and compassion, we can also enhance our own lives. The title underlines his positive message that the hurt can be healed and is a line from the prayer of St Teresa of Avila and whenever I'm fearful or apprehensive I remind myself of her thoughts:

"Let nothing disturb you,
Let nothing affright you,
All sorrows pass,
God alone remains,
All will be well."

ST TERESA OF AVILA

ॐ

Those words are like a comforting hand on my shoulder. And we've all been in situations where we think nothing could be this bad and things will never improve but they do. All will be well.

As well as visiting Kenya this year, I've travelled to Eritrea, Ethiopia, Liberia, Malawi, and Tanzania. Compared to the people who dedicate their lives to improving the quality of life for people in these countries, I've done miniscule amounts of work. It has been a pleasure for me to meet so many Africans who, in spite of the enormous poverty and hardship that they endure, have always moved me with their warmth, their friendly welcome and their joyous nature. What's fascinating is that they maintain their gentility, warmth and joy in the face of the harrowingly difficult circumstances in which they live. I love to spend time with them and am grateful for the wake up call they give me about what's really important in life.

You get a good idea of their humour and their spirituality in these words of Archbishop Desmond Tutu:

> *"When the white missionaries came to Africa,*
> *they had the Bible and we had the land.*
> *They said: "Let us pray."*
> *We closed our eyes.*
> *When we opened them*
> *We had the Bible and they had the land."*
> ARCHBISHOP DESMOND TUTU

ॐ

You don't need me to tell you that African people have a great sense of rhythm and music. They love to sing and they love to dance. One of my greatest pleasures on my trips to Africa is to go to a church service. For a start the churches are packed with all age groups. The liturgy is always uplifting, punctuated by so many voices singing beautiful harmonies. The children dance and everybody sways to the music. When you leave at the end, you could be walking on air.

The same is true of their parties, sing-songs or get-togethers. Everyone is welcome. There's singing, dancing and lots of laughter. I have treasured memories of sitting on a verandah in Kenya last April, late at night, in almost total darkness (the generator had failed), listening to a Kenyan woman singing 'Malaika'.

ॐ

"Malaika, nakupende malaika.
(Angel, I love you.)
Malaika, nakupende malaika."

ॐ

It's a love song, as well known in Kenya as Ireland's 'Danny Boy'. *Malaika* is the Swahili word for Angel. The man declares his love for his angel and says he would like to marry her but he has no money:

"Pesa zasumbua roho yangu."
(Money is troubling me.)

ॐ

The song is very beautiful, incredibly melodic, full of gentleness and simplicity – like the African people as a whole.

It's a privilege to go to Africa and to partake in different projects to improve conditions for the people. I'm aware though that there is a school of thought that feels "what's the point?". "The problem is huge." "The governments are corrupt." "It's just a drop in the ocean." "Why bother?"

When I'm faced with those reactions I remind myself of the beliefs of two people who lived their lives in the service of their fellow human beings. One is Mother Teresa of Calcutta, who said that her calling was to be "God's love in action to the poorest of the poor". Whenever someone attempted to point out to her that the situation was overwhelming and impossible, she replied:

"Don't think about numbers.
Just help one person at a time."
MOTHER TERESA OF CALCUTTA

The second person who refused to be discouraged by other people's negativity and sense of hopelessness when facing the magnitude of the difficulties of people's lives in his own country was Mahatma Gandhi.

He said:

"When I despair, I remember
that all through history
Truth and love have always won.
There have been tyrants and murderers,
And for a time they can seem invincible,
But in the end they always fall.
Think of it. . . always."

MAHATMA GANDHI

ॐ

Truth and Love – what wonderful aspirations for this world we live in.

 For Africa we do well to remember the words of Nelson Mandela, spoken in Pretoria in May 1994 at his inauguration as President of the Democratic Republic of South Africa.

ॐ

"The time for healing of the wounds has come.
The moment to bridge the chasms that divide us has
come.
The time to build is upon us . . .

ॐ

Let there be justice for all.
Let there be peace for all.
Let there be work, bread, water and salt for all.
Let each know that for each, the body, the mind and the soul
Have been freed to fulfill themselves . . .

ॐ

Let freedom reign.
The sun shall never set on so glorious a human achievement!
God bless Africa!"

NELSON MANDELA

ॐ

"A Thing of Beauty"

"I wandered lonely as a cloud,
That floats on high o'er vales and hills
When all at once I saw a crowd
A host of golden daffodils."

WILLIAM WORDSWORTH

ॐ

I often wonder why it is that everybody you meet can recite those lines. If they know no other line of poetry whatsoever, the chances are still high that they will know those first four lines of Wordsworth's "Daffodils". Whatever the reasons, and I'm sure they differ from person to person, I think one thing's for sure – we can all relate to the joy that Wordsworth felt when he happened on that host of daffodils. We all welcome the return of colour into our gardens, our parks and even our motorways, when the daffodils and the other spring flowers emerge after the dull days of winter. It's true that every season has its place and its charm. Stanley Horowitz, the American author and engineer, well known for his interest in energy and the environment, was certain of that anyway:

> *"Winter is an etching,*
> *Spring a watercolour,*
> *Summer an oil painting,*
> *And Autumn a mosaic of them all."*
>
> STANLEY HOROWITZ

ॐ

I can see what he means. And it's nice to have the seasons described in artistic terms because Nature is certainly the most beautiful piece of art we're likely to experience. In this instance though, I can live without the etching of winter.

I love the Spring. It gives me a real sense of hope and renewal. It's an optimistic time of the year and that optimism is conveyed in a lovely sentence from Margaret Elizabeth Sangster's poem "Awakening".

ॐ

> *"Never yet was a springtime when the buds*
> *forgot to bloom."*
>
> MARGARET ELIZABETH SANGSTER

ॐ

Every February I feel optimistic, full of plans and projects. Isn't it great that a few flowers can have that effect? These are the words of Rachel Carson, the American writer and ecologist who had a life long love of nature and the living world, which she inherited from her mother.

༄

"Those who contemplate the beauty of the earth find reserves of strength that will endure as long as life lasts. There is something infinitely healing in the repeated refrains of nature – the assurance that dawn comes after night, and spring after winter. "

RACHEL CARSON

༄

It works for me anyway. But then I love gardening and every type of garden. I like visiting gardens and just soaking up the atmosphere unique to each one. I'm lucky, because working on *Nationwide* has given me the opportunity to visit some very beautiful gardens around the country. This summer, for instance, I spent a lovely afternoon filming in Salthill Gardens, a place full of colour and wonderful growth. We were there in June and the scent of the roses was wafting on the air. Elizabeth Temple, who created the gardens, has always made a point of only growing roses with a scent. The place is delightful. You'll no doubt assume these gardens are in County Galway, but no, Salthill Gardens are actually just outside Mountcharles, which is a few miles from Donegal town. Well worth a visit if you're in the area.

The gardens of Bantry House are also lovely. I was there when the Angel's Fishing Rods were in full bloom and there is nothing more delicate. Even the name is pretty.

Giving slips from my garden to friends and receiving some from theirs is another great pleasure. I like looking at those slips as they grow and remembering the person who gave them to me. I hope they do the same. Isn't it nice to be remembered that way? I also like talking about flowers and gardening although I'm no expert and know very little about the more unusual flowers but that's okay. As Elizabeth Lawrence said in her book *Through the Garden Gates*:

> *"I love being asked to identify plants, and I don't know which gives me more pleasure: to know what they are or not to know what they are."*
>
> Elizabeth Lawrence

৶

Not knowing makes me want to find out. And like everything in life, once I come across something for the first time, it seems afterwards as if it's everywhere. I suppose I become more observant once my curiosity has been aroused. And it's only fair to say that when it comes to flowers, I'm always curious. I just can't get enough of them. As Dorothy Parker, in one of her gentle moments, said:

"Flowers are Heaven's masterpiece."

DOROTHY PARKER

ॐ

It's true. There is nothing nicer than the colour, the different shapes and forms, and of course the scent, of a nicely filled flowerbed. Robert Bridges, the medical doctor turned writer, who was poet laureate in England from 1913 and who died in 1930, referred to the scent in a garden in one of his best known works, "Testament of Beauty".

ॐ

"I know that if odour were visible, as colour is, I'd see the summer garden in rainbow clouds."

ROBERT BRIDGES

ॐ

It's not just in flowerbeds that I appreciate flowers and find them enriching either – I like buying flowers for friends and also for myself. Well for my house, not so much for myself! I don't mind spending money on them either. I'd be of the same school of thought as Emma Goldman, anarchist and major figure in the history of American feminism.

ॐ

"I'd rather have roses on my table than diamonds on my neck."

EMMA GOLDMAN

ॐ

Flowers lift my spirits and as well as buying roses for my table I also spend money on flowers and plants for my garden. Gardening is hard physical work but it's so satisfying and gives a nice feeling of achievement. In the Spring I like to get out into the garden to get it ready for planting. The soil has to be turned and freshened-up and the weeds have to be cleared. James Russell Lowell, the nineteenth century poet and US Ambassador to England from 1880 to 1885, was of the opinion that:

"A weed is no more than a flower in disguise."

JAMES RUSSELL LOWELL

ॐ

I admire his benign disposition towards weeds but I show no such mercy. Although I do recite that line as I uproot the weeds and consign them, hopefully, to oblivion! Recognising the dreaded weeds takes time also. Some of them have a knack of disguising themselves by growing with tiny blossoms and it's only later, when they become big and tough and are choking the plants that the penny drops. I read once that the best way to be sure whether it's a weed or a valuable plant is to pull it. If it comes out easily, it is, or rather was, a valuable plant!

 Weeds aside, I'm not always crazy about the digging. Depending on my energy levels, my back sometimes takes longer to straighten after a session with the spade than at other times. I wonder could that be anything to do with advancing years and a back that has been bending and digging for too many years now! I know I'm not alone with this difficulty. As far back as 1871, Charles Dudley Warner in his book, *My Summer in a Garden*, declared:

> *"What a man needs in gardening is a cast-iron back, with a hinge in it."*
>
> CHARLES DUDLEY WARNER

ॐ

I do relish the actual turning of the soil though. I feel as if I'm airing the flower beds in just the same way as if I was opening the windows and airing a room. It's a nice feeling but it takes a lot more effort than opening a couple of windows! I understand though what John Steinbeck meant when he said:

"There is nothing pleasanter than spading when the ground is soft and damp."

JOHN STEINBECK

ॐ

Mind you, he was probably glad of the opportunity to get a break from the typewriter when he was pouring over *The Grapes of Wrath* for instance. Like I said, physical tiredness is a much more pleasant situation than mental fatigue. I was pleased when I came across that quote from Steinbeck. So many people of his academic and literary inclination would have shunned such dirty physical work! I think it's such a pity when that happens. Look at what Mahatma Gandhi, a man of great wisdom and insight, had to say about it.

ॐ

"To forget how to dig the earth and to tend the soil is to forget ourselves."

MAHATMA GANDHI

So I must continue to dig and look forward to a relaxing bath afterwards as my reward. I'm joking of course – the smell of the freshly turned earth, the weed free beds and the rejuvenated looking garden are their own reward. On the other hand, I suppose I could take the writer Charles Barr's advice about gardening.

৯

*"The best way to get real enjoyment out of the garden
is to put on a wide straw hat,
dress in thin loose-fitting clothes, hold a little trowel in
one hand and a cool drink in the other, and tell the
man where to dig."*

CHARLES BARR

৯

Not for me though. I like the work. I plant my flowers, I water them and feed them and I mow the lawn. I think the garden looks great when the grass is cut. Just as I disagree with James Russell Lowell on weeds, I take issue also with one Michael Pollan's harsh words, written in his 1991 publication, *Second Nature:*

"A lawn is nature under totalitarian rule."

MICHAEL POLLAN

Be that as it may, I will be continuing the reign of totalitarianism with my lawns, back and front.

And when the work is done and the garden is tended, I get great pleasure from just sitting in it. There are different bits of garden furniture all around my garden and they are perfectly positioned in the various spots where the sun shines (when it shines!) at different times of the day. Down in the far corner I read the paper and have coffee in the morning. And as the sun moves around during the day there is always a comfy chair and a little table where I sit and enjoy each new perspective. I finish up at the dining table and chairs, just outside the kitchen door, which get the last rays of the sun and where I love to have dinner with family and friends. I have little white lights in the trees and just before I go to bed I like to go down to the corner that gets the morning sun and sit there. The house lights and the treelights throw shadows around the garden. It's a time when I can relate fully to what James Douglas had to say in *Down Shoe Lane.*

ॐ

"It is good to be alone in a garden at dawn or dark so that all its shy presences may haunt you and possess you in a reverie of suspended thought."

JAMES DOUGLAS

ॐ

For me it's a quiet time. It's peaceful and silent in the garden at night-time. I'm sorry but I cannot comment on whether the same is also true of the garden at dawn!

I know that Jane Austen favoured the daytime peace of the garden.

ฬ

"To sit in the shade on a fine day and look upon verdure is the most perfect refreshment."

JANE AUSTEN

ฬ

What a lovely gentle thought. It wouldn't work in my garden. During the day there's a cacophony of sound, especially with Patch, the dog, barking at any aeroplanes that dare to pass overhead. Patch is still trying to enforce a no-fly zone over our house. Oscar, the older cat, fighting with Maggie, the younger, is another distraction. That's not to say, however, that I don't enjoy sitting there among them all, doing nothing and enjoying the garden. I'm getting better at that.

I like to throw off the sandals or shoes and feel the grass under my feet. As Kahlil Gibran said in *The Prophet:*

"And forget not that the earth delights to feel your bare feet and the winds long to play with your hair."

KAHLIL GIBRAN

ॐ

I used to always feel the need to be doing something, even if I was supposed to be sitting and relaxing. I have a piece of paper on which I've written some lines which remind me of the need to slow down.

ॐ

"We spend most of our lives conjugating three verbs; to want, to have and to do.
But none of these verbs has any ultimate significance until it is transcended by and included in the fundamental verb – to be."

EVELYN UNDERHILL

ॐ

How right she is. Evelyn Underhill was a spiritual writer and a pacifist and certainly her advice in these lines about "being" makes a lot of sense. We do hear a fair bit of talk these days about the need to "be present in the moment" and if the moment is about just sitting and enjoying a garden, then I want to do just that.

I'm not a total sloth though. I do like to be active as

well and I've started walking fast for exercise. Up to this year I ran and jogged for that reason but I've had trouble with Quad Tendinitis. Roughly translated, that means that my right knee is giving me the same message I get from my back after a day digging in the garden! I'm getting into the walking now. It takes a bit longer than a run but it has its merits. It's a great opportunity for thinking and clearing the head without the interruption of the pain and the exertion of running. Henry David Thoreau, for whose writings I have a great affection, said of walking:

"Methinks that the moment my legs begin to move, my thoughts begin to flow."

HENRY DAVID THOREAU

ॐ

And some wonderful thoughts he had too, full of insight and wisdom. The fact that he's still read and admired almost 300 years after he was born is fair testimony. I'm not for a moment suggesting that I have thoughts like Thoreau but I do like to mull over things when I'm out walking. I can never understand why some people, when they're out walking or running, are wired for sound with their ipods in place. I would never be tempted to listen to music or the radio while I'm out walking. For me it's a time for ruminating and planning. It's when I deal with whatever is troubling my head at that particular time. As St Augustine remarked:

"Solvitur ambulando; it is solved by walking."
ST AUGUSTINE

ॐ

It's also a time for toning and being diligent about fitness and not putting on excess weight. When I was forced to stop running I was worried that the weight would be a problem but I've found that walking is an excellent exercise and tones the body well. There's a very funny line written by the British sportsman Chris Adams that I came across in a book on physical fitness.

ॐ

"People say that losing weight is no walk in the park.
When I hear that I think,
Yeah that's the problem."
CHRIS ADAMS

ॐ

It took me a while to figure out what he was getting at. The problem of course is that the people who moan about how difficult it is to lose weight are not doing the walk in the park!

85

It shouldn't just be about walking with an end in sight though. The walk can be its own reward. It's so nice to be outdoors, breathing the air and taking in the surroundings. We all feel better about ourselves and our world after being out and about. It gives the happy hormones a chance to do their work. Well, most of us feel better about ourselves after a bit of fresh air. Fran Lebowitz is an exception however. She believes that:

"The Great Outdoors is what you must pass through in order to get from your apartment to a taxicab."

FRAN LEBOWITZ

ॐ

One of the nicest descriptions of the joys of the Great Outdoors that I've ever come across was written by John Muir. It refers to mountain climbing but I think it can equally be applied to hill walking, jogging or even a leisurely walk in the park.

ॐ

"Climb the mountains and get their good tidings. Nature's peace will flow into you as sunshine flows into trees. The winds will blow their own freshness into you and the storms their energy, while cares will drop off like autumn leaves."

JOHN MUIR

I do have a special feeling for Nature and I always enjoy time in the country and being out in the natural environment but as well as that, I'm a city person, born and bred in Clondalkin and still living in Dublin. I like the buzz of the city, the people, the theatres, the restaurants, the concert venues, and the buildings. I like the fact that I can be in O'Connell Street in thirty minutes depending on the time of day of course. The fact that it can take longer at other times is a fact of city life. It's something that has to be factored in. As the American lawyer, the late Robert N Davis Jr put it, in his *Buffalo Issue Alerts:*

"Everyone claims to want a city, but no one wants city living. City living, by its definition, is crowded. It is tolerant of other people. It is dependent on a sophisticated population that makes a hundred compromises daily so that they can benefit from the collective energy that a city generates."

ROBERT N DAVIS JR

I'm a fan of that collective energy you get in a city and I make the compromises to be able to live in Dublin. Perhaps that's why I like to visit other cities and experience their energy, their architecture, their culture and their compromises. I love to visit Paris and stroll along the boulevards and listen to the people conversing in French while they sip their wine *au moment de l'apéritif.* That's their equivalent of our pint after work! Prague is another favourite of mine, for the splendour of its architecture and the beauty of its opera at affordable prices. You can enjoy a wonderful evening at the magnificent State Opera House for a very modest amount of money, which includes a glass of champagne at the interval. And then there's New York, New York – so good they named it twice – the buzz, the buildings, the people, the neon lights on Times Square, Saint Patrick's Cathedral on 5th Avenue. Oh and did I mention the shopping?!

Of course there are times when I like to get out of the city and into the countryside. I like the scenery, the freedom, the freshness and the wildness of the countryside here in Ireland and in other countries as well.

ॐ

> *"What would the world be, once bereft*
> *Of wet and wildness? Let them be left,*
> *Let them be left, wildness and wet:*
> *Long live the weeds and the wilderness yet."*
>
> GERARD MANLEY HOPKINS

That's what the poet had to say about the countryside around the river Inversnaid in Scotland. I agree with him. Even about the weeds – as long as they're not in my flowerbeds!

My sister, Deirdre, lives on Inis Mór, the largest of the Aran Islands and it's a rugged, unspoilt landscape. Its rich in reminders of our ancient heritage and also in examples of our modern culture, language, music and dance. I love to spend time there and there's a poem by Máirtín Ó Direáin that epitomises the peace and beauty of island life there. It's called "An tEarrach Thiar", (Spring in the West).

❧

> *"Fear ag glanadh cré*   *A man cleaning the earth*
> *De ghimseán spáide,*   *From the tread of the spade*
> *Sa gciúnas séimh*   *In the gentle quiet*
> *I mbrothall lae:*   *Of the heat of the day:*
> *Binn an fhuaim*   *A sweet sound*
> *San Earrach Thiar*   *Of Spring in the West"*
> MÁIRTÍN Ó DIREÁIN

❧

And so we've come full circle. This piece began with an excerpt from "The Daffodils", a celebration of spring. The joys of "spading" as John Steinbeck referred to it were extolled and also Rachel Carson's contemplation of the earth. It's exactly the same in this Irish poem about Spring in the West. All those elements are present. It's a universal truth that Nature is a thing of beauty and as John Keats told us:

> *"A thing of beauty is a joy forever."*
> JOHN KEATS

I think it's fitting to leave the final words here to Rachel Carson because they sum up nicely the joy and the beauty of Nature.

ॐ

"It is a wholesome and necessary thing for us to turn again to the earth and in the contemplation of her beauties to know of wonder and humility."

RACHEL CARSON

Inspirational Women

"I have become my own version of an optimist.
If I can't make it through one door,
I'll go through another door—
Or I'll make a door.
Something terrific will come no matter how dark the
present."

JOAN RIVERS

ॐ

If I had asked you to guess who wrote those lines, I believe you'd be a long time coming up with the right answer. The message is thoughtful, positive, determined, self-reliant and aware of the fact that life has its dark moments. It's not a message that you would necessarily associate with the American comedienne Joan Rivers, a woman who makes jokes about everything under the sun, including cosmetic surgery, problem children, bad sex, ageing and even her husband's death by suicide. Nothing is taboo. She's sharp, witty and very funny.

Here's one of her milder jokes:

"I hate housework. You make the beds; you do the dishes. And six months later you have to start all over again."
JOAN RIVERS

ॐ

That's more like the Joan Rivers we know from the television. When I came across the other serious piece a few years ago, I kept it. Why? I liked the message. I found it motivational. And I liked the fact that it came from this woman who comes across as very funny, flippant and without a care in the world. Appearances can be so deceptive and while she's definitely a funny woman, she's also, judging by those words, a woman with spirit and character, who's prepared to meet adversity head on and overcome the obstacles in order to move to "something terrific". There are other women like that who've captured my imagination over the years and I love to collect sayings and lines about them and by them.

One of the earliest books I remember reading by myself, once I'd gone beyond having fairy tales read to me at bedtime, was the story of Florence Nightingale. Boy, did she capture my imagination. I can still remember the picture of her on the cover. It was a thin hardback Ladybird book, a first reader kind of edition. I was probably about six or seven years old. The cover had a blue background and Florence, the Lady with the Lamp, was leaning over a wounded soldier. He had a bloody bandage on his head and a pained expression on his face. I didn't realise it then but she was a woman prepared to speak her mind.

☙

"No man, not even a doctor, ever gives any other definition of what a nurse should be than this – "devoted and obedient." This definition would do just as well for a porter. It might even do for a horse. It would not do for a policeman."

FLORENCE NIGHTINGALE

☙

I love it! Florence had a tongue on her as they say.

Nursing was not seen as quite respectable in her day. She was from a comfortably well-off family and when, in 1837, at the tender age of 17, she told her family she had heard the voice of God telling her she had a mission in life and that mission was nursing, they were not best pleased. However, Florence followed the voice and became a pioneer in the field of nursing during the Crimean War. My book concentrated on that war. I was fascinated by the exotic location, hadn't a clue where Turkey was but I read the story over and over, until the book finally fell apart. For me, Florence was gentle and kind, very pretty, a romantic figure. I did, however, absorb the fact that her insistence on hygiene had cut the death rate in the field hospital, although they didn't include her quite caustic comments on the issue in my little reader!

ও

"It may seem a strange principle to enunciate as the very first requirement in a hospital, that it should do the sick no harm."

FLORENCE NIGHTINGALE

ও

I wonder what she'd have to say about some of our modern hospitals. I reckon she'd take on the old MRSA question with gusto!

ও

Florence died in 1910 and all through her life she worked for the improvement of the health service. She was also a champion of women and their contribution to society. I'd say this next piece will strike a chord with a lot of women. It was written in 1852. Some things just don't change!

*"Women never have a half-hour in all their lives
(excepting before or after anybody is up in the house)
that they can call their own, without fear of offending
or of hurting someone. Why do women sit up so late,
or, more rarely, get up so early? Not because the day is
not long enough, but because they have 'no time in the
day to themselves'."*

FLORENCE NIGHTINGALE

ॐ

As time moved on, I progressed from first readers to more weighty tomes. I remember one Christmas being given a copy of *The Water Babies* by Charles Kingsley. It's about a young chimney sweep who eventually ends up living underwater in a magical world. I didn't like it at all. I must have started it a dozen times. I don't remember what happened in the end. Maybe I didn't finish it. I was never much of a fan of fantasy and make believe, always preferring stories based in the real world. That's probably why I loved Florence Nightingale and why, even now, I prefer reading biographies and factual books to most fiction.

I was fascinated by the story of Joan of Arc. I first came across her history when I was about 12 years old.

I learnt off her last words as she was being burnt at the stake and can still remember them:

"My voices did come from God and everything that I have done was by God's order. Hold the crucifix up before my eyes so I may see it until I die."

JOAN OF ARC

ᘏ

I think my interest in Joan had something to do with the fact that she was only a few years older than me when she led the French army against the English towards the end of the Hundred Years War. It was incredible to think that she also oversaw the coronation, in Reims, of Charles VII as King of France. All this when she was just 17 years of age! Later, Joan was captured, handed over to the enemy, tried and convicted of heresy. She was burned at the stake in Rouen in 1431, when she was just 19. When she died, Jean Tressard, who was secretary to the King of England, declared:

"We are all ruined, for a good and holy person was burned."

JEAN TRESSARD

ᘏ

Joan went on to be beatified in 1909 and canonised, by Pope Benedict XV, in 1920.

George Bernard Shaw wrote a play called "Saint Joan" and I was happy to have to learn pieces from it for Speech and Drama (sorry Elocution!) exams but my favourite piece about her is a poem written by William Wordsworth who described her beautifully.

&

"A perfect woman, nobly plann'd,
to warn, to comfort, and command;
And yet a spirit still and bright
With something of an angel light."
WILLIAM WORDSWORTH

&

Little Women was a must for young girls in my day. We loved the story of the sisters and we all had our favourites. My mother loved it too. I think all mothers did in those days and there was great excitement when the black and white movie version came on the television. Louisa May Alcott's lovely use of English and the subtleties in the text went way over my young head, no doubt, but I had occasion to re-read the book in the not too distant past. When my mother was spending her last days in Tallaght Hospital in the winter of 2001, I happened on a copy of *Little Women* while I was in the local library with my children. It caught my eye immediately and I borrowed it. I read excerpts from it to my mother when it was my turn to keep her company. My brothers, sister and I had worked out a roster, which meant that Mam had one of us by her side at all times. I was so impressed by one particular piece I read that I brought it in to work the next day and photocopied the page and have kept it ever since. It's from the chapter "Meg Goes To Vanity Fair" and in this piece Mrs March is spelling out her dreams for her daughters.

ॐ

"I want my daughters to be beautiful, accomplished, and good; to be admired, loved, and respected, to have a happy youth, to be well and wisely married, and to live useful, pleasant lives, with as little care and sorrow to try them as God sees fit to send."

LOUISA MAY ALCOTT

ॐ

 Certainly, the aspirations are of their time. *Little Women* was first published in 1868. All the same, isn't that what we all want for our daughters (and our sons as well of course)? We want them to be happy and fulfilled, without too much trouble in their lives. Mrs March goes into some more detail and finishes her speech with a lot of common sense:

"My dear girls, I am ambitious for you, but not to have you make a dash in the world – marry rich men merely because they are rich, or have splendid houses, which are not homes because love is wanting. Money is a needful and a precious thing – and when well used, a noble thing – but I never want you to think it is the first or only prize to strive for. I'd rather see you poor men's wives, if you were happy, beloved, contented, than queens on thrones, without self-respect and peace."

LOUISA MAY ALCOTT

჻

Apart from that being a lovely piece of gentle, motherly writing, it's undoubtedly got a lot of wisdom in it as well. There are a few situations in today's materialistic world which could do with a dose of Mrs March's logic!

There are two other books, one about a woman and the other written by a woman, which greatly influenced me as I was growing up. I loved the story of Amelia Earhart, pioneer in aviation. She was the first woman to fly solo across the Atlantic, taking off from Newfoundland in May 1932 and landing in 'Gallagher's pasture' in Derry. She received many awards following that flight. President Hoover presented her with a gold medal from the National Geographic Society and Congress awarded her the

Distinguished Flying Cross. She felt the flight proved men and women were equal in:

"jobs requiring intelligence, coordination, speed, coolness and willpower."

AMELIA EARHART

༊

My Dad bought me that book and I was enthralled by this woman who had such courage. Back in the 1930s, she was certainly blazing a trail. Amelia Earhart was a risk taker and enjoyed the challenge.

༊

"Adventure is worthwhile in itself."

AMELIA EARHART

༊

When I wrote my first book *Paper Tigers* a few years ago, it was from something Amelia Earhart said that I got the title. I remember that piece so well. Her words are reassuring, positive and inspirational.

"The hardest thing is the decision to act. The rest is merely tenacity. The fears are paper tigers. You can do anything you decide to do. You can act to change and control your life; and the procedure, the process is its own reward."

AMELIA EARHART

ॐ

I suppose the same message is contained in the Nike ad nowadays: "Just do it."

Amelia Earhart was a woman of courage and vision. She loved the adventure of flying but she also had an appreciation of the simple aspects of life as well.

ॐ

"The effect of having other interests beyond those domestic works well. The more one does and sees and feels, the more one is able to do, and the more genuine may be one's appreciation of fundamental things like home, and love, and understanding companionship."

AMELIA EARHART

ॐ

In 1937, as Amelia was approaching her 40th birthday, she set out to be the first woman to fly solo around the world. She almost made it but her plane disappeared over the Pacific and her body was never found.

Amelia Earhart always fascinated me. She was a strong woman, a risk taker, a champion of women's right to live life the way they want. Her last letter to her husband before she set out on that fateful flight shows that.

ॐ

"Please know that I am aware of the hazards. Women must try to do things as men have tried. When they fail, their failure must be a challenge to others."

AMELIA EARHART

ॐ

 Another book from my childhood that had a lasting impact on me was *Uncle Tom's Cabin* by Harriet Beecher Stowe. I read it when I was about 12 and the reason I was drawn to it was because I had an Uncle Tom and he lived next door. Simple as that! Little did I know what lay between its covers. Once I started reading it, I couldn't put it down. Not surprising really when you consider that it was the biggest selling book in the nineteenth century, second only to the Bible.

Harriet was a Connecticut born teacher working at the Hartford Female Academy. She was so incensed by the passage of the Fugitive Slave Law in 1850, which punished those who helped runaway slaves, that two years later she wrote this anti-slavery novel from the point of view of three black slaves, Tom, and a married couple, Eliza and George. Other characters in the story are Little Eva, Topsy and the horribly cruel slave owner, Simon Legree. The brutality was horrific, the humanity enthralling and the slaves dialect completely authentic. I felt I was there with them.

꩜

"Yes Eliza, it's all misery, misery, misery! My life is bitter as wormwood; the very life is burnin' out of me. I'm a poor miserable forlorn drudge."

HARRIET BEECHER STOWE

꩜

I cried buckets while I was reading *Uncle Tom's Cabin* and have no doubt I would again were I to read it now. It's a powerful novel. My mother had an expression that intrigued me as a small child. If something was left lying about and nobody would take responsibility, she used to say:

"I suppose it just 'growed' there, like Topsy!"

꩜

I hadn't a clue what she was talking about until I read *Uncle Tom's Cabin*. Topsy is a bright young slave girl who came out with more than one funny expression.

Her answer to one particular question is what gave my mother her Topsy moment.

❧

"'Do you know who made you?'
'Nobody as I knows on,' said the child, with a short
laugh.
The idea seemed to amuse her considerably;
for her eyes twinkled and she added—
'I 'spect I growed. Don't think nobody never made me.'"

HARRIET BEECHER STOWE

❧

I love the wide-eyed innocence that I visualise when I read those lines and the sweetness of the child. And I also like the fact that it's where my mother's retort has its roots. And guess what? I use it in exactly the same context in my house, with my children.

And yes, you're right – they do look at me as if I've lost the plot!

When Abraham Lincoln met Harriet Beecher Stowe nine years after the publication of her novel, at the start of the American Civil War, in 1861, he is reputed to have said:

"So this is the little lady who made this big war."

ABRAHAM LINCOLN

Well done, Harriet. She brought about change in her own way. But she was always a woman of conviction. It wasn't just the question of slavery that interested her as you can see from some of her other writings, which I've collected over the years and have included in other parts of this collection. I like her sensible no-nonsense approach to life.

Her reaction to being asked about her championing the cause of the Negro slave epitomises this.

ༀ

"It's a matter of taking the side of the weak against the strong, something the best people have always done."

HARRIET BEECHER STOWE

ༀ

All these amazing women have helped to inspire me because as many of us learn through life:

"Optimism is the faith that leads to achievement. Nothing can be done without hope."

HELEN KELLER

ༀ

And their achievements have made it easier for me to understand that:

"Happiness is not a state to arrive at, but a manner of travelling."

MARGARET LEE RUNBECK

Making Honey

"Last night as I was sleeping,
I dreamt- marvellous error!-
that I had a beehive
here inside my heart.
And the golden bees
were making white combs
and sweet honey
from my old failures."

Antonio Machado

❧

This poem, "Last Night As I Was Sleeping", was written in 1903 by the Spanish poet Antonio Machado and was translated into English by Robert Bly. I came across it a few years ago in a collection called *Ten Poems to Change Your Life*. I was seeing a counsellor at the time and it was she who recommended the book. Now we all know that no one sees a counsellor when they are feeling on top of the world. Rather one seeks help when one is at a loss, or a crossroads or a low ebb.

I got a lot of consolation from reading the poems in that book but Antonio Machado's stood out. I love the image of the bees making sweet honey out of my failures. What a positive and uplifting thought that good can come from bad. Nice things can follow on difficult times. We need to remember that and to believe it in order to overcome the obstacles in our path and move forward. Those lines have become my mantra since I discovered them. I say them to myself when I feel a bit down, insecure or unsure. They remind me that we need to forgive ourselves. We are our own harshest critics.

ॐ

"Admit your mistakes, then move on."
THOMAS MERTON

ॐ

Sometimes that's easier said than done. The timing has to be right. I have to feel ready to move onwards and upwards. My confidence has to go up a notch or two. Certainly those lines about the bees inside my heart making honey from my failures helps in that regard.

We all have our good days and bad days, after all it's part of the human condition. And as we grow and mature, we realise that nobody escapes the bad days. Some people would have us believe that they live very straight-forward lives; that they sail through without turmoil, difficulties, sadness or worry. I don't believe them for a minute. I accept there are people who feel the need to pretend that life is a bowl of cherries. I think that façade just adds to the pressure when times are tough. It's so much healthier to admit that, at different times, and for different reasons, life can be hard. Harriet Beecher Stowe had words of comfort for people as they encounter grief along the path of life.

ॐ

"Any mind that is capable of real sorrow is capable of good."

HARRIET BEECHER STOWE

ॐ

I agree with that. All the experiences we gather along the way are absorbed and contribute towards making up the whole of who we are. The sadness and the turmoil in our lives make us more compassionate and aware of other peoples' difficulties. They make us appreciative of happy moments and of the comfort of friends.

ॐ

"I think somehow, we learn who we really are and then live with that decision."

ELEANOR ROOSEVELT

ॐ

Learning from all these experiences doesn't happen overnight though. It takes time to feel that the bees are making honey from our failures. It's nice to have other people's considered words though to help us along the road to that realisation. That's why I like reading poetry. I love the insight the words give into the poet's feelings and the poems I prefer, are the ones that I can read and then say to myself, "yes, I know that feeling".

Brendan Kennelly's poem "I See You Dancing, Father" is a good example.

ॐ

"You're buried now
In Lislaughtin Abbey"

BRENDAN KENNELLY

ॐ

His father is dead but the son chooses to remember happy times when his father was dancing, whistling, making music. The tone is positive. The time of sadness has passed.

ॐ

"Your lips are enjoying themselves
Whistling an air.
Whatever happens or cannot happen
In the time I have to spare,
I see you dancing, father."

BRENDAN KENNELLY

My Dad died 30 years ago this year. At the time I felt I would never recover from the grief I felt at his passing. When he died of a heart attack on the golf course, I can still vividly remember how it felt; so sudden and so unexpected. Time does heal the broken heart though and now I remember the happy times when he was alive and his great sense of fun. That's how I remember him now and reading Brendan Kennelly's poem was a great comfort as I realised that other people remember their fathers the way I remember mine.

I haven't got to that stage with regard to my mother. She's not yet six years dead so it will take a bit longer before I remember the happy times. The loneliness and the sadness at her passing are still uppermost. Perhaps that's why, when I read Patrick Kavanagh's poem about his late mother, I can sense the loneliness and the huge sense of loss he feels even though he conjures up lovely images of when his mother was alive.

ॐ

"And I think of you walking along a headland
Of green oats in June,
So full of repose, so rich with life."
PATRICK KAVANAGH

ॐ

There's no doubt this is a bright happy picture Kavanagh paints of his mother walking in the summer. Unlike Brendan Kennelly's poem though, there's an underlying note of loss and sadness here. For a start, there's the mention of:

"the wet clay of a Monaghan graveyard."

ॐ

And the fact that:

"Among your earthiest words the angels stray."

ॐ

Also, as Kavanagh and the others are piling up the ricks at harvest time:

"And you smile up at us-eternally."

ॐ

In those three lines, I get a huge sense of longing and loss. It's not something that I feel in Brendan Kennelly's equally lovely poem about his father. But maybe it's just me and where I am with regard to my own feelings around the passing of my father and more recently my mother. Whatever the truth of the matter, I have great affection for both those poems and I take them out from time to time because they bring my Mam and Dad right back into my life.

There are lots of other poems that I like for the different situations and feelings they evoke. Pádraic Colum wrote a very well known poem "The Old Woman of the Roads". She's a woman who has no home, is wandering the roads and fantasising about having a place of her own.

ॐ

"Oh to have a little house!
To own the hearth and stool and all!
The heaped-up sods against the fire,
The pile of turf against the wall!"

PÁDRAIC COLUM

ॐ

I learnt that poem a long, long time ago but it's come back into my life recently. Even though it was written a hundred years ago I think it has a message for us in this very wealthy society in which we live. Last January I was compere at a conference organised by people in the property business and I quoted those opening lines at the start of the proceedings. I wanted to use them as an indicator of how far we had come in this country in a relatively short space of time. The poem is also a good reminder of the fact that most Irish people want to own their own home. Times are changing certainly and there are apartment blocks going up all over the country, but at the end of the day, we, unlike other Europeans, like to own our piece of land with a house and a garden. It's part of our cultural legacy I suppose, because we were a dispossessed people for so many centuries. The Irish poet Máirtín Ó Direáin put it very plainly in his poem "Stoite" (Uprooted).

❧

Thóg an fear seo teach	*This man built a house*
Is an fear úd clai no fál	*That man a hedge or a fence*
A mhair ina dhiaidh	*That lived on after him*
Is a choinnigh a	*And kept his memory alive.*
chuimhne buan.	
Sinne a gclann	*We their children*
Is clann a gclainne,	*And their children's children*
Dúinn is éigean	*We are compelled*
Cónaí a dhéanamh	*to live*
In árais ó dhaoine	*in flats belonging to people*
A leagfadh cíos	*who would look for*
Ar an mbraon anuas .	*the last drop of rent.*

MÁIRTÍN Ó DIREÁIN

❧

These days, in the new prosperous Ireland, houses are selling for millions and millions of euro. It's not so long ago though that people were forced to emigrate in search of work and to live in rented accomodation owned by greedy landlords.

There were many who would echo the words of Colum's old woman:

"To have a clock with weights and chains,
And pendulum swinging up and down!
A dresser filled with shining delph,
Speckled with white and blue and brown!"

PÁDRAIC COLUM

ঽ

The difficulty these days is the high price of houses. I'm thinking of my own children who are beginning to emerge into the world of work and adult living. They have a tough road ahead when they try to get on the property ladder. I don't know how young people manage to scrape together the deposit for their first home. Perhaps, we'll be hearing echoes of the sentiments in this poem again in years to come.

ঽ

"And I am praying to God on high,
And I am praying him night and day,
For a little house-a house of my own-
Out of the wind and the rain's way."

PÁDRAIC COLUM

ঽ

I made reference to "The Old Woman of the Roads" at another function I was at during the year and something really sweet happened. There was a home-making theme to the event and when I said the first couple of lines as far as "the hearth and stool and all", the people in the audience joined in. Okay, so they were of an age where they would have learnt the poem in school but they were happy to say it and afterwards a lot of people said it brought them a moment of nostalgia, back to their childhoods and learning poetry. The simplicity of the poem is very appealing. All the woman aspired to was a roof over her head, turf on the fire and a few simple possessions. How far our aspirations have now moved in spite of still being such a young country! The danger nowadays is that the emphasis is on the grandeur of the house and its contents. Certainly, it's nice to have beautiful things. It's important though to remember that it's the atmosphere and the values that make a home. There's a very sound piece of advice in *The Prophet* when he talks about houses and what they should contain.

"Have you remembrances, the glimmering arches
that span
The summits of the mind?
Have you beauty, that leads the heart from things
fashioned
Of wood and stone to the holy mountain?
Tell me, have you these in your houses?
Or have you only comfort, and the lust for comfort,
that
Stealthy thing that enters the house a guest, and then
becomes
A host, and then a master?"

KAHLIL GIBRAN

ॐ

As Robert J Wicks remarked in his book *Everyday Simplicity, A Practical Guide to Spiritual Growth*:

"This sense of peace is the real hospitality we need to
offer people when they come into our lives. . .
Hospitality is not simply being "chronically nice" to
strangers. Instead, it is offering others a gentle space
where they can feel
welcomed for who they are now."

ROBERT J WICKS

ॐ

And that can just as easily happen, whether people are sitting on an orange box or on a top of the range leather settee. Simplicity is the key – like the old woman of the roads in Pádraic Colum's poem.

I think it's a pity there isn't the same store placed in schools nowadays on learning and saying poems aloud.

I have very fond memories of my grandmother saying poems for us when we were young. She never went further than Primary school but she could quote Shakespeare to beat the band. Her favourite poem to say for us was Oliver Goldsmith's "The Village Schoolmaster". She'd ask how school was going and then she'd say things were different long ago and she'd begin:

> *"Beside yon straggling fence that skirts the way*
> *With blossom'd furze unprofitably gay,*
> *There, in his little mansion, skill'd to rule,*
> *The village master taught his little school."*
>
> OLIVER GOLDSMITH

Those are the opening four lines and there are twenty-two more to follow. "The Village Schoolmaster" is actually an excerpt from a longer piece called "The Deserted Village". Granny probably knew all of that too! When you consider that she left school after Primary level it means that she had amassed that store of lovely words and images by about 12 years of age. Her tone would become very serious when she'd get to these lines!

༄

"A man severe he was, and stern to view,
I knew him well, and every truant knew;
Well had the boding tremblers learn'd to trace
The day's disasters in his morning face…"

OLIVER GOLDSMITH

༄

Granny lived to be 102 and she recited poetry and pieces of Shakespeare all the time. One of her favourite pieces was from *Hamlet* where Lord Polonius is giving financial advice to his less than thrifty son.

༄

"Neither a borrower nor a lender be,
For loan oft loses both itself and friend
And borrowing dulls the edge of husbandry."

WILLIAM SHAKESPEARE

༄

Then she'd explain the meaning of the piece, encouraging us to save money and not be "beholden to anybody!" What a lovely gift she has though and what lovely memories she has given me and all her other grandchildren.

ॐ

"And still they gaz'd and still the wonder grew,
How one small head could carry all he knew."

OLIVER GOLDSMITH

ॐ

You could wonder the same of my grandmother I suppose. She, and others of her generation, got great pleasure from the lovely language, imagery and rhythms of poetry. It was the same when I was growing up and we actually learned poems in school. I don't have the same memory that my grandmother had but I do still like to read those poems aloud. I don't think my children will have that pleasure. In these sophisticated technology driven times, the spoken word has lost some of its appeal. And as for learning something off by heart – sure that went out with the button boots!!

There is one poem that I learned in school that I can remember bits of to this day. It's T S Eliot's epic, "Love Song of J. Alfred Prufrock" which was on the Leaving Cert course. Not an easy poem by any means and I have memories of analysing it to within an inch of its life in English class. The norm at the time was to learn extracts off so they could be used in the exam and I loved the sounds of that poem from the opening lines.

ↄ

"Let us go then, you and I,
When the evening is spread out against the sky
Like a patient etherised upon a table;
Let us go, through certain half-deserted streets,
The muttering retreats
Of restless nights in one-night cheap hotels
And sawdust restaurants with oyster-shells..."

T S ELIOT

ↄ

If my memory serves me correctly, the "you and I" are Prufrock's inner and his outer self. There's wonderful imagery through the poem with echoes of Dante's "Inferno", shadows like cats, crabs creeping, mermaids singing and of course all the sleazy back street references. It's full of sadness and regret for the type of life he's lived. I loved dissecting that poem but most of all I loved the way it sounded and the way the pace and the rhythm changed from time to time.

"Shall I part my hair behind? Do I dare to eat a peach?
I shall wear white flannel trousers and walk upon the
beach.
I have heard the mermaids singing, each to each.
I do not think that they will sing to me."

T S ELIOT

ॐ

To finish off this chapter, I have to end with a piece by a poet I love, Patrick Kavanagh. For me, the Monaghan man has a wonderful ability to paint pictures with words. This poem is called "Peace" and it conjures up a lovely rural setting that Kavanagh knew well and loved as he was growing up. He swapped that for the city life in Dublin but in these lines, there's a longing to be back there.

ॐ

"And sometimes I am sorry when the grass
Is growing over the stones in quiet hollows
And the cocksfoot leans across the rutted cart-pass
That I am not the voice of country fellows
Who are now standing by some headland talking
Of turnips and potatoes or young corn
Or turf banks stripped for victory.
Here peace is still hawking
His coloured combs and scarves and beads of horn."

PATRICK KAVANAGH

He continues to describe the simple, earthy rural simplicity of life and then there's the question at the end which holds the tinge of regret for having forsaken that wholesome life.

ॐ

"Out of that childhood country what fools climb
To fight with tyrants Love and Life and Time."

PATRICK KAVANAGH

ॐ

Kavanagh comes across as vulnerable in those lines. The fact that he called the poem "Peace" shows me a longing on his part for something that he imagines and remembers from his past and which eludes him in Dublin. We all long for the idyllic pastoral setting from time to time, especially when we have to struggle in our busy daily lives.

I say those last two lines to myself when I'm feeling overwhelmed or stressed. I acknowledge my vulnerability but it's nice to know that others have been in the same boat!

"It is a Sweet Thing Friendship"

"And in the sweetness of friendship let there be laughter,
And sharing of pleasures.
For in the dew of little things the heart finds its morning and is refreshed."

KAHLIL GIBRAN

ॐ

What a beautiful description of friendship there from Kahlil Gibran – I love those lines and think of them often. They underline for me the joy and the pleasure of true friendship but they also pinpoint the fact that its pleasures and its value lie in the simple non-materialistic realms of our lives.

How right he is. Money, wealth, fancy material acquisitions can sometimes bring comfort, excitement, ease of worry but unless they are kept in perspective and a person has a strong foundation of family and especially friends behind them, these material things are just that – things.

As the writer Mark Twain once said:

*"To get the full value of joy you must have somebody
to divide it with."*

MARK TWAIN

ॐ

These thoughts are further illustrated in this very simple line from the French writer Antoine de Sainte-Exupery, author of *Le Petit Prince*.

ॐ

"There is no hope of joy except in human relations."

ANTOINE DE SAINTE-EXUPERY

ॐ

It's a funny thing, however, that although we all have friends, it's an area of our lives that we don't tend to talk about much. While I was reading through some quotes I have collected about friendship, it struck me, that through the years, I haven't discussed the qualities of friendship in the same way that I would discuss the qualities of motherhood, of marriage, of death, of work, of success and failure or of anything else really. And with whom am I having these discussions about everything under the sun bar friendship?

With my friends of course!

It's bizarre when you think about it. Is it because friendship is an innate part of our lives or is it because we take friends for granted? The French writer Francois de la La Rochefoucauld pondered this question back in the seventeenth century.

ॐ

"A true friend is the most precious of all possessions and the one we take the least thought about acquiring."
FRANCOIS DE LA LA ROCHEFOUCAULD

ॐ

We fall into friendship, from the time we start playing on the road with neighbours, to progressing through the stages of school friends, college friends and on to work friends. One stage follows another. When we think back over those life stages though and remember the important moments, whether they were happy or sad, funny or serious, the presence of friends was an essential element of what made those moments memorable. With that realisation in mind I think it might be nice to reflect for a moment on the gift of friendship, its qualities and its responsibilities.

Isn't it interesting that a lot of the maxims about friendship are light-hearted?

Take Groucho Marx for instance and his take on friendship.

૨

"Outside of a dog, a book is man's best friend.
Inside a dog, it's too dark to read."

GROUCHO MARX

૨

And we're probably all familiar with the fridge magnet that says:

"You'll always be my friend. You know too much."

૨

I like the bright and breezy tone of those two quotes. They reflect the fun we can have with friends. We accept our friends and they accept us, virtues and failings alike, because, as Mother Teresa always believed:

"If you judge people, you have no time to love them."

MOTHER TERESA OF CALCUTTA

૨

Henry Brooks Adams had the same philosophy but a different way of expressing it!

ॐ

"Every man should have a fair-sized cemetery
In which to bury the faults of his friends."
HENRY BROOKS ADAMS

ॐ

A friend is somebody we can unburden ourselves to without fear of judgement or disapproval. A friend will listen to our problems because they want to help. They will offer advice and support. And we will listen in turn to their worries and offer advice and support, without judgement. For me that's the essence of true friendship.

Watching my children make friends, just as I had done a generation before them, reminded me of how early we make friends. As soon as they were old enough to play on the road, start Montessori school, then Primary and then Secondary they were finding friends. Some of those friendships have endured, others haven't. All were valuable, special and very spontaneous. As we get older though, and we move on to work and marriage and new families, we become slaves to time and different commitments. That's when it's easy to neglect friendships. The pressures of just

127

living day by day can be all-consuming. Sometimes there's just no time for anything else. And yet it's true friends who can help us in these pressurised times. Only if they're still around though, and we haven't "lost touch", as they say.

ॐ

"Go often to the house of thy friend,
For weeds choke the unused path."

Ralph Waldo Emerson

ॐ

That's how the American writer and philosopher Ralph Waldo Emerson put it in the nineteenth century and it's as true today as it was then.

There is a need to nurture our friendships. Every Christmas I feel guilty as I write cards to friends I've known down the years and used to see from time to time until our mutual circumstances changed, for one reason or another. "Where does the time go?" we all ask and there's no doubt we lead busy lives dictated by tight schedules. Every year though, as I write those Christmas cards, I resolve to get in touch in the New Year. And then the New Year arrives and I slip back into my routine of work, family, close friends, projects and so on and so on. It's a pity really to lose touch with people we like and whose company we enjoyed and would continue to enjoy if we met them again. It's a shame because we are fundamentally communicative beings who thrive on human interaction. Abraham Lincoln believed this to be true.

ॐ

"The better part of one's life consists of his friendships."
ABRAHAM LINCOLN

ॐ

Lincoln is not the only well-known person to espouse the importance and the value of maintaining and nurturing friendships. As Robert Louis Stevenson said:

"No man is useless while he has a friend."
ROBERT LOUIS STEVENSON

ॐ

Our friends give us love, support and advice when we need it. They lift our spirits and enhance our self-esteem. And it's a two-way street. We do the same for them. Friends are there for each other. They offer a listening ear and a shoulder to cry on and that's a comforting thought in life.

It would be wrong though if we only invested time and energy in our friendships in times of need. Of course this can happen sometimes but the end result is that one half of the friendship ends up feeling used. There's an imbalance which needs to be redressed. We should follow the advice of The Prophet as he talks of friendship.

ॐ

"And let your best be for your friend.
If he must know the ebb of your tide, let him know the
flood also.
For what is your friend that you should seek him with
hours to kill?
Seek him always with hours to live."

KAHLIL GIBRAN

ॐ

I like those lines because they really do sum up the responsibility of good friendship. There's no doubt about the great comfort of having a friend to turn to at the ebb tide, when times are tough but we must also let our friends share the flood – the times of joy. And we must be able to share in their triumphs without any hint of envy or jealousy. I think it was Gore Vidal who said that whenever he heard of a friend's success, something inside him died. It does happen. In fact I came across a piece about friendship in my mother's copybook that dealt with this.

"The only certain test by which we can ascertain our sincerity towards our friends is the feeling with which we receive the news of their happiness or their rising in the world, especially if Fortune has raised them a degree above our own level."

ANON

ৎ

My mother was a woman who put great store by friendship. She had many friends from different periods of her life and she kept in touch with them always. As a child I looked forward to the nights she would be having "the girls" around for supper. The girls were Mollie, Cherry, Joan and Connie, three women she had worked with in the College of Science and a fourth who knew them all. Mam would spend the day making sandwiches, an apple tart, a sponge cake and maybe butterfly buns. These would all be served on china plates with doyleys. And the tray, with her best china cups and saucers, would be laid in advance in the dining room. If it was during the winter months she'd light the fire in the sitting room and pull the couch and the armchairs in closer to the hearth. The girls would all arrive together and they'd spend the evening chatting and laughing and catching up.

There was a great sense of joy and warmth about those gatherings. The friendships had endured many years, with lots of happy and sad times along the way. They gave their best to each other. I came across a poem about friendship in my Mam's copybook called

"The Joy of Friends" and I can see why she chose it, as it reminds me of the way she valued her friends.

ॐ

"It is my joy in life to find
At every turning of the road
The strong arm of a comrade kind
To help me onward with my load;

FRANK DEMPSTER SHERMAN

The last two lines really say it all.

ॐ

"My only prayer is, while I live –
God make me worthy of my friends."

FRANK DEMPSTER SHERMAN

ॐ

My mother held her friends in high regard and the reverse is also true. After she died I was moved by the number of people who told me stories about kindnesses my mother had shown them, advice she had given, secrets she had kept; things we as children knew nothing about. She was a loyal friend who showed compassion and understanding always. It was after I got this insight into my mother's dealings with her friends that I understood the significance of another piece about friendship she had included in her copybook. It's a poem called "Can't We Understand" by Jean Morton. The first two lines set the scene.

ॐ

*"Oh can't we understand those little faults
Like flaws within the splendid life of friends."*

JEAN MORTON

ॐ

The poem goes on to give various examples of the struggles we all encounter in life and the closing lines are magnanimous and compassionate.

ॐ

*"So can't we understand the losing fight,
They have put up and gone down in the end.
Oh can't we understand all this and more.
Understanding proves ourselves a friend."*

JEAN MORTON

ॐ

There's no doubt our friends are an incredibly important part of our lives. We are thinking, feeling human beings who need interaction with others in our lives. There's an old Irish proverb:

"Is ar scáth a chéile a mhaireann na daoine."

AN IRISH PROVERB

श्र

It bears the same message as these lines:

"No man is an island entire of itself
Every man is a piece of the continent, a part of the
main."

JOHN DONNE

श्र

This is not to imply that we don't all need time on
our own, moments of solitude and quiet but these
times don't take away from the importance and
loveliness of good friendship.

One of my favourite quotes about friendship was
written by the poet Percy Bysshe Shelley who
encapsulates the beauty and the joy of friendship.

श्र

"It is a sweet thing friendship, a dear balm,
A happy and auspicious bird of calm."

PERCY BYSSHE SHELLEY

श्र

Can't you feel the comfort of those lines? It's just like
the comfort of a good friend.

Mother Teresa of Calcutta

"At the end of life we will not be judged by how many diplomas we have received, how much money we have made, how many great things we have done. We will be judged by "I was hungry and you gave me food; I was naked and you clothed me. I was homeless and you took me in."

MOTHER TERESA

ॐ

Those are the words of Mother Teresa who dedicated her life to the poor people of Calcutta. She called them "the poorest of the poor" and she was right.

I travelled to Calcutta twice and there's no hiding the squalor and the abject poverty. The city is about the same size as Dublin yet it has a population of 18 million people, five million of whom live on the streets, many of them children. Take a drive through the streets of Calcutta, day or night, and your jaw will drop. People sleep everywhere, under bridges, on the pavement, on piping and on cardboard. I saw three young boys, aged about 14, huddled together asleep without any cover, much less shelter, against the rain. It was Monsoon season. I saw groups of children, some of them toddlers, crouched over the rubbish dumps looking for scraps of food, or bottle tops and rubber bands. Anything they could sell.

I was reminded of a famous line from Isadora Duncan.

ও

"So long as little children are allowed to suffer, there is no true love in this world."

ISADORA DUNCAN

ও

There's no shortage of suffering in Calcutta. I visited an orthopaedic hospital for children with physical deformities. I saw everything from club foot and polio to disease-induced deformities. One little boy came to meet me on his knees because his lower legs had formed backwards. He'd been rescued from the railway station. I was told he was reluctant to have the operation to correct his condition because he was afraid he'd make less money begging if his legs were straight and he could walk.

I visited the red light district to see the homework clubs run for children of prostitutes so they have somewhere to go while their mothers are working. Otherwise the children are in the room at the time as there's only one room in Calcutta's hovels. The mind boggles and not just at the thought of a small child lying quietly under the bed while his or her mother is with a client. Violence is often a feature of those sexual encounters.

As I walked through the streets, I was propositioned by a young girl. I was surprised until it was pointed out to me that the money's the same and there's less chance of violence with a woman. Walking through the streets of Calcutta's red light district is like walking through a guard of honour. The women line both sides of the street. They stand shoulder to shoulder because there are hundreds of them and some are as young as 13 years of age. These are Mother Teresa's people. She lived among them and cared for them. She also brought their plight to the attention of the world. She was awarded the Nobel Peace Prize in 1979 and her acceptance speech illustrates her dedication.

ॐ

"I choose the poverty of our poor people. But I am grateful to receive [the Nobel] in the name of the hungry, the naked, the homeless, of the crippled, of the blind, of the lepers, of all those people who feel unwanted, unloved, uncared for throughout society, people that have become a burden to the society and are shunned by everyone."

MOTHER TERESA

Of course there are many organisations working in Calcutta on behalf of the poor and destitute. The trip that I've described above was my second visit and it was with GOAL. The hospital and the homework clubs I visited are run by GOAL, as are the half-way houses for boys and girls who have been rescued from the streets. They also run the drop-in centre over the wall from Sealda railway station, for children who live on its platforms and need some respite from its depravity.

John O'Shea, who founded GOAL 30 years ago this year, was a friend and supporter of Mother Teresa's. He always called to see her when he was visiting the city. I suppose she inspired him to commit his energies to what many would describe as an utterly hopeless situation.

And what inspired her to take on such a task? It's true she was a nun and had a religious vocation.

ॐ

"By blood and origin I am Albanian. My citizenship is Indian. I am a Catholic nun.
As to my calling, I belong to the whole world.
As to my heart, I belong entirely to the heart of Jesus."

MOTHER TERESA

ॐ

Not every nun though would be able for the awfulness of Calcutta. It was Mother Teresa's special calling:

*"The dying, the cripple, the mental, the unwanted, the
unloved - they are Jesus in disguise."*

MOTHER TERESA

❧

Mother Teresa trained as a Loreto nun in
Rathfarnham in Dublin, before going out to teach in
Calcutta. When she saw the destitution there she was
moved to start her own order, The Missionaries of
Charity. Their express function was to care for the
poor, the dying and the shunned. These sisters walk
the streets of Calcutta in their white saris, with blue
stripes, seeking out the people who need their care
and their love. Love was something that Mother
Teresa stressed always in her dealings with people.

❧

*"It is not how much we do, but how much love we put
in the doing. It is not how much we give but how
much love we put in the giving."*

MOTHER TERESA

❧

The proof of that was borne out for me by the
reaction of the people of Calcutta when she died. My
first visit to the city was in September 1997. I was
sent over to provide the RTÉ commentary at Mother
Teresa's funeral which came at the end of a week of
grieving among the Christian and non-Christian
communities. There were mile-long queues, day and
night, outside Saint Thomas's church while she lay in

state. As the people filed past her remains, they cried, prayed, kissed her feet, lifted small children to touch her robes and left flowers by her side. There were billboards, banners and posters all over the city with messages on them. For instance:

"We mourn for the loss of our Mother."

❧

After the funeral, I was amazed to see old and frail Hindu women kneeling on the streets, praying in front of cardboard boxes that they had made into little shrines to Mother Teresa. They covered the boxes with satin and bedecked them with incense sticks and had little nightlights shining in front of pictures of Mother Teresa. Her image held pride of place on these simple little altars. This was their way of marking her passing and honouring the contribution she had made to the lives of all the people of Calcutta, regardless of their creed. If they were poor, hungry or ill, she was there to minister to their needs. That was her *raison d'être* if you like, her reason for living.

❧

"Unless a life is lived for others, it is not worthwhile."
MOTHER TERESA

❧

I know there are those who would say it was easy for Mother Teresa to live that way because of her calling to the religious life. There are others, though, who echo that belief. Nobody could accuse the French writer and women's campaigner Simone de Beauvoir of having a calling to the religious life and yet among her writings I was pleased to come across a very similar philosophy to that of Mother Teresa.

༉

"One's life has value so long as one attributes value to the life of others, by means of love, friendship, indignation and compassion."

SIMONE DE BEAUVOIR

༉

Mother Teresa fits the bill on all counts. She gave love, friendship and compassion to the poor and destitute always and she showed indignation at the injustice manifest in their plight.

༉

"I try to give to the poor people for love what the rich could get for money. No, I wouldn't touch a leper for a thousand pounds, yet I willingly care for him for the love of God."

MOTHER TERESA

༉

It's important to remember that India is a country that can afford nuclear weapons, has the fastest growing technology industry in the world and has huge food reserves. Mahatma Gandhi, known as "the father of the nation," was the symbol of the Indian struggle for independence, the 60th anniversary of which independence the country is celebrating this year. He is revered the world over as having been a man of great peace and wisdom. This is what he had to say about India's wealth.

❧

"In this, as in all the countries of the world, possession of inordinate wealth by individuals should be held as a crime against Indian humanity."

MAHATMA GANDHI

❧

 During my second visit to Calcutta, with GOAL, I had occasion to visit a slum area down by the port. It was the nearest thing to hell on earth that I had ever seen. I was shocked and so was the Indian camera crew with me. They live in Calcutta and yet they didn't realise the extent of the squalor, poverty and misery that exists in that slum. We picked our way through absolute filth. We passed mud huts, canvas shelters, lean-tos covered in plastic sheeting, down muddy, filthy, narrow passageways. This was home to 2,000 people.

The assault on the senses was extreme. The stench was nauseating. There's no sanitation in this slum of

2,000 souls. I could feel the smoke from the fires, burning in oil drums, sticking to my clothes. As I pulled my feet out of the sludge and mud, I could see rats scurrying into the sides of the alleyways. Rats and wild pigs, with their piglets, snouting around in the dirt are the order of the day here. At one point the rain was falling like stair rods and I was soaked to the skin. I was quite literally stuck in the mud when a rat ran in front of me. I stood there and a feeling of utter helplessness swept over me. I felt like crying. How could anybody have to live like this in the 21st century, in a country that is not poor? These people don't have enough to eat, yet in order to reach the slum you pass fully-stocked grain stores at the entrance to the port. The Indian government will have nothing to do with them because they are illegal migrants from the neighbouring province of Bihar. Not that they do anything to alleviate the poverty of the people who were born and bred in Calcutta either. They have this very useful religious philosophy that insists that the poor lived bad former lives and this horrific existence is their way of wiping the slate clean for their future lives. Mother Teresa's answer to official stone-walling was succinct.

ॐ

"Do not wait for leaders. Do it alone, person to person."

MOTHER TERESA

ॐ

And so she did. The poor people of Calcutta regarded her as their champion. She cared for them and, as well as that, she respected them.

※

"The poor give us much more than we give them. They're such strong people, living day to day with no food, and they never curse, never complain. We don't have to give them pity or sympathy. We have so much to learn from them."

MOTHER TERESA

※

The dignity of the person was something that was paramount in Mother Teresa's dealings with the poor. She recognised their strength of character and refused to be patronising.

She became a world figure who spoke out on numerous occasions, on behalf of the destitute and the dying. On her travels though, she saw that the affluent world was not without its problems.

※

"In the West there is loneliness, which I call the leprosy of the west. In many ways it is worse that our poor in Calcutta."

MOTHER TERESA

※

I witnessed at first hand the abject poverty to which millions of people in Calcutta are subjected. I stepped over sleeping bodies on the street. My heart went out to groups of men gathered around water troughs at five am, with their little plastic dishes carrying a bar of soap and a toothbrush. These grown men were standing in the teeming streets, lathering their bodies before throwing a bucket of cold water, from the same trough, over themselves to rinse away the soap. Women were filling billy-cans with water which is poured into the gutters in the early morning to wash away the previous day's filth. They then boiled this water over gas stoves to make tea. I felt overwhelmed and very helpless initially. I felt so sorry for these people. And yet everywhere I went, I was greeted by warm, smiling and friendly faces. These people had nothing but they remained quietly dignified, hospitable and very welcoming. A sharp contrast to some of the travails of the west for sure. Mother Teresa put her finger on it when she said:

"We think sometimes that poverty is only being hungry, naked and homeless. The poverty of being unwanted, unloved and uncared for is the greatest poverty. We must start in our own homes to remedy this kind of poverty."

MOTHER TERESA

ॐ

She was an astute woman all right. Mother Teresa wasn't fooled by the affluence of our world. She could see that wealth and prosperity bring their own problems and that they are worth nothing if there is no spiritual and emotional wellbeing.

ॐ

"Let us not be satisfied with just giving money.
Money is not enough, money can be got,
but they need our hearts to love them.
So spread your love everywhere you go."

MOTHER TERESA

ॐ

I ran the gamut of emotions in Calcutta, from sadness and heartbreak, to sorrow and anger, and hope, love and joy. It's a place of desperate poverty, misery and filth. It's a place full of people who have nothing and who deserve so much, who are dignified, beautiful and hospitable. There's a saying in Calcutta that you can see God more easily there than anywhere else in the world. Maybe this is because the people are so dignified and spiritual in such awful circumstances. God's love is certainly manifest in the work of Mother Teresa, who died ten years ago this year, and in her Missionaries of Charity, who carry on that work. To finish this section, I have chosen my favourite words from Mother Teresa, which I think reflect the simplicity of her approach and the ripple effect of everything she did.

ॐ

"Kind words can be short and easy to speak,
but their echoes are truly endless."

MOTHER TERESA

A Twinkle in
Our Eye

*"So much has been said and sung of beautiful young girls;
Why doesn't somebody wake up to the beauty of old women."*

૪

This is what Harriet Beecher Stowe had to say about ageing. I wrote it in my notebook years ago when my grandmother was still with us. I think it marked the beginning of my awareness of the beauty of older women. Granny was elegant, serene, gentle and witty in old age. She always wore a necklace and a brooch. I remember as a child, wondering why she bothered going to all that trouble with her appearance. After all, she was old now. Then I came across that piece and it made me stop and think. Beauty is not just about youth.

I saw that in my mother also. She was just as beautiful and careful of her appearance in her later years as she had always been. She made a point of dressing up for occasions – getting the hair done, the make up on, with the jewellery, perfume, nail varnish all in place. As well as that though, I came to see the inner beauty that women have as they age. My mother had lovely thoughts; she was kind, generous and loyal. She felt for people who were in trouble or ill. She always held strong opinions and the strength of those opinions didn't diminish with age. Quite the opposite! I think it's a shame that the emphasis is on the young beautiful, almost to the exclusion of the older beautiful.

It's interesting that Harriet Beecher Stowe felt the need to comment on this subject during the nineteenth century and that it's still an issue in these modern times. It's a pity really because as Diana Cooper realised and proclaimed to us all:

> "Age wins and one must learn to grow old."
>
> DIANA COOPER

That's the truth of the matter. Wouldn't it be nice if we lived in a world where ageing quite simply didn't matter? Where there was no pursuit of the elixir of eternal youth, be it botox or the knife or whatever. Where everyone agreed, deep down in their hearts, with what Elizabeth Arden had to say and let's face it she earned her living from the beauty business.

"I'm not interested in age.
People who tell their age are silly.
You're as old as you feel."

ELIZABETH ARDEN

ॐ

Mind you, not all women have such self-confidence. The French writer, Collette, had a funny line about how she looked, which is quite telling.

ॐ

"Give me a dozen such heartbreaks
If that would help me lose a couple of pounds."

COLLETTE

ॐ

I'm presuming she was being facetious. She was, after all, of the opinion that:

"Total absence of humour renders life impossible."

COLLETTE

ॐ

I have always liked collecting quotes and I tend to have a lot that were written by women. I suppose that's because I relate to the issues that exercise the minds of other women. And it's comforting to realise that even very well known and well regarded women share the concerns of us mere mortals. Take Marie Curie, for instance. She was a pioneer, along with her husband Pierre, in researching radioactivity and was the first person to win a second Nobel prize. She is also the only person who is mother of another Nobel prize winner, her daughter, Iréne Joliot Curie. When Marie Curie's husband died suddenly, she refused a pension and took his place as Professor at the University of Paris. Pretty impressive portfolio and yet she comes across as quite a humble person.

ॐ

"We must never forget that when radium was discovered, none knew that it would prove useful in hospitals."

MARIE CURIE

ॐ

She seems to have been quite a sensible person as well. Her Nobel prize-winning daughter said of her:

*"That one must do some work seriously, must be independent and not merely amuse oneself in life –
this our mother taught us always, but never that science was the only career worth following."*

IRÉNE JOLIOT CURIE

ॐ

You would be forgiven for thinking that somebody like Marie Curie had life under control. After all, she won the Nobel prize not once, but twice and then one of her two daughters followed in her footsteps and won it as well. Listen, however, to what she had to say about juggling home and work.

ॐ

"I have frequently been questioned, especially by women, of how I could reconcile family life with a scientific career. Well, it has not been easy."

MARIE CURIE

ॐ

As I said, it's comforting to know that women like Marie Curie didn't find it easy either. Another good example of this is Golda Meir who was Prime Minister of Israel from 1969 to 1974. She was born in the Ukraine and grew up in the United States, from where she emigrated with her husband to Palestine. When Israel won independence, Golda Meir was the only woman appointed to the first cabinet. She was a woman of some wit.

ॐ

"We have always said that in our war with the Arabs we had a secret weapon ...no alternative!"

GOLDA MEIR

ॐ

And it wasn't only with regard to the struggle between the Jews and the Arabs that she made such comments. She was just as witty about her own kind.

Let me tell you something that we Israelis have against Moses. He took us 40 years through the desert in order to bring us to the one spot in the Middle East that has no oil!"

GOLDA MEIR

Like the writer Collette, she could see the value of humour.

"It's no accident many accuse me of conducting public affairs with my heart instead of my head. Well, what if I do?… Those who don't know how to weep with their whole heart, don't know how to laugh either."

GOLDA MEIR

So, here we have this strong, positive woman who came out of retirement to lead the Labour Party and who became Prime Minister of her country at the age of 71. How did she fare, juggling family life with work?

"At work, you think of the children you've left at home. At home, you think of the work you've left unfinished. Such a struggle is unleashed within yourself, your heart is rent."

GOLDA MEIR

We can all relate to those sentiments. I came across another example of a strong woman when I was in Kenya last Easter. She's Wangari Maathai, the Deputy Minister for the Environment and Natural Resources. I'd seen her photo in the newspaper while I was there and picked up her autobiography in Nairobi. The title, *Unbowed,* gives a good insight into the type of woman she is.

Wangari was born in 1940 and grew up in Ihithe, a rural Kenyan village, at a time when most African girls were uneducated. Her love of the countryside and rural living from the time she was a child is obvious. She used to cultivate the soil with her mother when she was small.

ॐ

"Although the work was hard, it was rewarding. Because of the frequent rainfall, the soil of the central highlands was often wet enough so that you could make a ball with it, but still porous and smelling fresh. When you rubbed it between your fingers you could almost feel the life it held."

WANGARI MAATHAI

ॐ

Can't you just sense the love she had for the soil? Wangari was determined to improve her situation though and was educated first by Catholic missionary nuns. She studied in the United States as well.

"Coming to New York city was like landing on the moon."

WANGARI MAATHAI

Her time in the States came about as part of the Kennedy Airlift scheme. As Kenya became independent, nearly 600 of the country's young people were funded to study in different colleges and universities in the US. On her return, Wangari became the first woman in East and Central Africa to earn a PhD and the first woman to head a university department in Kenya. During the mid-seventies she became involved in politics and founded the Green Belt Movement which spread from Kenya across Africa. It helps restore indigenous forests, while improving the lot of rural women by paying them to plant trees in their villages.

Wangari's life was one of struggle and hardship as she campaigned on environmental and human rights issues. Her story is fascinating. She had numerous runs-in with the corrupt government of Daniel arap Moi and spent time in prison and also under house arrest. She saw innocent people die. Her marriage broke up and she was separated from her children at times. I was amazed by her courage, tenacity and determination and delighted when in 2004, she was awarded the Nobel Peace Prize, in recognition of her:

"contribution to sustainable development, human rights, and peace."

ॐ

Wangari celebrated the announcement the best way she could – by planting a tree.

ॐ

"Trees have been an essential part of my life and have provided me with many lessons. Trees are living symbols of peace and hope. A tree has roots in the soil yet reaches to the sky. It tells us that in order to aspire we need to be grounded, and that no matter how high we go it is from our roots that we draw sustenance."

WANGARI MAATHAI

ॐ

Wangari Maathai continues to campaign for environmental awareness. The women of Kenya follow her lead and continue to plant seedlings in their villages. Future generations of Kenyans will be grateful she fought this cause. Their lives will be enhanced by the fact that one woman who loved the earth and its forests decided to make their conservation and restoration her life's work.

One of the most recent quotes I came across is relevant to the environment. It was on a poster in a cultural centre outside Newry in County Down. During the summer I was filming there for *Nationwide* and saw these lines attached to a notice board:

ॐ

I took out my notebook and jotted it down straight away. Who would have thought that I would see those words in a thatched cottage which is noted for storytelling, traditional Irish music and dance? I'm glad I did though. It's a sobering thought and a reminder of our responsibilities to the planet for the sake of future generations.

There's no doubting the fact that environmental issues must continue to top political agendas. We only have to look back on the summer we've had this year and the crazy weather patterns to realise that. There's another aspect of the question though that is also important. Raisa Gorbachev, wife of the former Soviet President Mikhail, has provided an interesting insight into another reason for environmental concern.

ॐ

An interesting perspective there from a woman who obviously feels strongly about the question. Her husband does also. He founded the global conservation organisation, Green Cross International. I must say though that Raisa's view point appeals to me. That's why I cut it out and kept it. I like the emphasis on the human values being intertwined with our treatment of the planet.

The women I've mentioned are all strong characters, not without humour and not without their difficulties. To finish this section, I've added a prayer that I think could be said by any of them, by all women in fact. It's from the pen of Margaret Bailey and it really sums up the qualities illustrated by the women I've mentioned – compassion, wisdom, courage, confidence and above all, that sense of fun.

"God, give me sympathy and sense,
And help me keep my courage high;
God, give me calm and confidence,
And – please – a twinkle in my eye."

MARGARET BAILEY

Would that we never, ever, lose that twinkle in our eye!

Oíche Nollag

"'Twas the night before Christmas, when all through the house
Not a creature was stirring, not even a mouse.
The stockings were hung by the chimney with care,
In hopes that St Nicholas soon would be there."

CLEMENT C MOORE

No marks for guessing what we're talking about here. That time of the year when we overspend, overeat and overstress. Christmas is also a time of tradition and a lot of hard work. I have to admit I take it a bit easier these days. I like Christmas and I'm a sucker for decorations and traditions but I refuse to get into a tizzy rushing around like a mad thing. When my children were small it was such a busy time, making sure all their wishes came true and that the magic was complete. The pressure was incredible. One Christmas, I had scouts looking for the turtle Donatello all over the country, north and south of the border. Some people don't seem to mind queuing for concert tickets or for the first day of the sales. I hate queuing but I've done it. I've camped outside toy shops when a rumour went around that a consignment of that year's favourite toy was due!

Now that my children are older, I enjoy the part of Christmas that means relaxation, taking it easy, carols in the church and calling on people that I haven't seen for ages. I still love the traditional aspects of the season though and before turning in on Christmas Eve I take out our copy of Clement C Moore's poem, "A Visit from St Nicholas" and read it aloud. There was a time when the children snuggled up and hung on my every word. These days, they're more likely to be wrapping presents, texting friends or just throwing the odd pitying look in my direction! I persevere though and relish the lovely illustrations in the book and the wonderfully descriptive words.

ও

"He had a broad face and a little round belly,
that shook when he laughed like a bowl full of jelly."

CLEMENT C MOORE

ও

The children used to giggle at those lines when they were young. Not any more obviously but I'd hazard a guess that when they have families of their own, the story of this *"chubby and plump, a right jolly old elf"* will creep back into their lives.

Although Clement C Moore's poem was written so long ago, in 1882 in fact, and published for the first time in a New York newspaper called *The Sentinel* on December 23, 1883, it was never a part of our traditions when I was growing up. Christmas Eve in Clondalkin was a day of many preparations and palpable excitement. The smells were of ham boiling, and onions stuffed with cloves simmering in milk for the bread sauce. The kitchen windows were steamed up because of the pudding bubbling away. I spent the afternoon sitting on a stool in the pantry because that's where the radio lived. I was listening to Santa calling out names from his list of Irish children.

Was my name ever called out? Never! And yet every year I sat there listening and hoping.

After tea and baths, it was time to put the candle in the window "to welcome baby Jesus and to let Mary and Joseph know that they could stay in our house". Dad would plug in the Christmas tree lights. I would play 'Silent Night' (a very simple version) on the piano and the youngest child in the family, Tony, would carry the lighted candle from the kitchen to the sitting room and place it on the window sill. The rest of the family would walk behind him, my mother at his shoulder in case he dropped the candle and set the place on fire! I love that tradition and continue to put a candle in the window over the Christmas holidays. They're few and far between now though. Time was when there'd be a candle in every window, on every road in all the towns and villages in Ireland. Máirtín Ó Direáin included the tradition in a poem he wrote at Christmas, 1942.

It's called "Cuireadh do Mhuire", (An Invitation to Mary).

ॐ

"Deonaigh glacadhh
Le cuireadh uaimse
Go hoileán mara
San iarthar chianda:
Beidh coinnle geala
I ngach fuinneog lasta
Is tine mhóna
Ar thealllach adhanta."

"Please accept
An invitation from me
To an island in the sea
Over in the distant west;
There will be bright candles
Lighting in every window
And a turf fire
Lit in the hearth."

MÁIRTÍN Ó DIREÁIN

ॐ

Máire Mhac an tSaoi also refers to this lovely Irish tradition in a poem she wrote called "Oíche Nollag" (Christmas Eve).

ॐ

"Le coinnle na n-aingeal tá an spéir amuigh breactha,
Tá fiacail an tseaca sa ghaoith ón gcnoc,
Adaigh an tine is téir chun na leapan,
Luífidh Mac Dé ins an tigh seo anocht."

MÁIRE MHAC AN TSAOI

"With candles of angels the sky is speckled,
There's a biting frost in the wind from the hill,
Bank the fire and go to bed,
The Son of God will sleep in this house tonight."

As well as the candle lighting in the window Máire Mhac an tSaoi also refers to leaving the door ajar so that the Holy Family will sleep in the house. Both of those poems were on the Secondary School curriculum when I was a teacher and I always made a point of teaching them just before the Christmas holidays. They went down very well with the girls and I still love the images they evoke; the candles in the window and the fire lighting. They're simple and welcoming and, while the emphasis is on the religious aspect of Christmas, the overriding feeling is of the humanity of the situation. I like that.

That's not to say that I don't relish all the religious aspects of Christmas. The church ceremonies are so appealing. I love the crib, the poinsettia plants on the altar, the holly wreaths along the pillars, the carols and the readings about the Nativity. All of this is central to the celebration of Christmas. I wouldn't be part of the Bart Simpson school of thought:

"Aren't we forgetting the true meaning of Christmas —
the birth of Santa!"

ॐ

From the beginning of Advent, four weeks before the birth of Jesus, there's a special atmosphere in the church. There's a sense of preparation even though there's no austerity associated with Advent these days, no fasting for instance, as there was in times past. Patrick Kavanagh has a lovely poem called "Advent" which celebrates the fact that during Advent, while we're preparing for Christmas, there's an opportunity to appreciate afresh the important things in life, an opportunity to cut back on the luxuries that we take for granted during the year.

ॐ

"We have tested and tasted too much, lover –
Through a chink too wide there comes in no wonder."

PATRICK KAVANAGH

ॐ

It's a pity when life is so full of material concerns that we lose sight of the wonder of simple pleasures. Advent gives us a chance to redress the balance.

ॐ

"…in the Advent - darkened room
Where the dry bread and the sugarless tea
Of penance will charm back the luxury
Of a child's soul…"

PATRICK KAVANAGH

ॐ

What a nice thought, especially when you consider the innocence and honesty of a child's soul and the excitement they feel in the run up to Christmas.

ॐ

"And Christ comes with a January flower."

PATRICK KAVANAGH

Now that's as good a description as any, of the true meaning of Christmas. That January flower, the Christmas rose, is white and bright in the dark of winter.

That poem is a part of the sounds of Christmas for me now. I came upon it a few years ago and it hit the spot. It encapsulates the spirit of Christmas as I was saying I like to celebrate it now, taking things quietly, seeing friends and going to carol services.

The sounds of Christmas past fall into two categories; when I was a child and when my own children were small.

As a child the carols were important. We learnt them in school and sang them at Mass on Christmas morning.

ॐ

"Away in a manger, no crib for a bed,
The little Lord Jesus laid down his sweet head."

TRADITIONAL

ॐ

And when we came home from Mass there was the excitement of Santa and the presents and Christmas dinner with the cousins next door. Uncle Tom was a great man for coming out with songs that would bring a lump to my throat. I've already told you that 'Scarlet Ribbons' was a favourite of his. Included in his Christmas repertoire was 'Little Drummer Boy', about the poor boy who went to visit baby Jesus in the stable and had no gift to bring. But he had the greatest gift of all.

ॐ

"I played my drum for Him, pa rum pum pum pum
I played my best for Him, pa rum pum pum pum,
Rum pum pum pum, rum pum pum pum,

Then He smiled at me, pa rum pum pum pum
Me and my drum."

DAVIS/ONORATI/SIMEONE.

ॐ

Yes, I know it's silly, but that always brought a tear to my eye. I know it's a happy song really but I got emotional every time Uncle Tom sang it. With that in mind, can you imagine my reaction when he started on 'The Little Boy That Santa Claus Forgot!' I'd be a blubbering heap in the armchair.

ॐ

"He's the little boy that Santa Claus forgot,
And goodness knows he didn't want a lot.
He sent a note to Santa for some soldiers and a drum;
It broke his little heart when he found
Santa hadn't come."

CONNOR/CARR/LEACH

ॐ

It broke my little heart as well, hearing about him. I was three years of age when Nat King Cole had a hit with that song but I cried whenever I heard it for many, many years after that. And as if Santa not coming wasn't enough…

☙

"In the street, he envies all those lucky boys,
Then wanders home to last year's broken toys
I'm so sorry for that laddie;
He hasn't got a daddy,
The little boy that Santa Claus forgot."

CONNOR/CARR/LEACH

☙

 Not that we were "bah humbug" type of people like Scrooge in Dicken's *A Christmas Carol*. Christmas was a very happy time. There were always plenty of treats and presents, although there were limits to what we got. Nobody was left like the little boy in the song above or indeed like Les Dawson used to say his Christmas was.

☙

"We were so poor that we couldn't afford a turkey.
We gave the budgie chest expanders.
It was five-aside to a cracker."

LES DAWSON

Television was a big part of Christmas. I loved Les Dawson's comedy programmes and Billy Smart's Circus in the afternoon. When I got older I looked forward to the Andy Williams Christmas Special before lunch. I'd watch it on my own as none of the others liked it. They'd be watching something on the telly next door. That was certainly one of the advantages of the two families living side-by-side. We had two televisions when no one else had! It was just me, Deirdre, Mam and Auntie Eilish for those Christmas specials. I was enthralled by Bing Crosby's *At Home* programme on Christmas Day. The fairisle sweaters, the huge Christmas tree, the snow outside and of course the singing.

❧

"I'm dreaming of a white Christmas
With every Christmas card I write,
May your days be happy and bright
And may all your Christmases be white."

IRVING BERLIN

❧

Isn't it amazing how evocative songs can be? From 'White Christmas' and 'Moon River', to 'Good King Wenceslas' and 'Once in Royal David's City', those Christmas songs are part of my children's Christmas memories as well. Like me, they learnt them at school. Unlike me, they performed them in their Nativity plays. We didn't have those in my day. A pity really because my children got great satisfaction from them, the moment they'd run in the kitchen door from school, announcing, "I'm Joseph in the play this year", or Mary or a shepherd or an angel. The excitement was great, the rehearsals diligent and the performance magical. I remember one particular year, at the end of the Nativity section of the evening, a line of seven year olds, my own among them, were all onstage for the finale, dressed in Santa hats. They recited with great gusto and enthusiasm:

"When Santa got stuck up the chimney,
He began to shout,
'You girls and boys,
Won't get any toys,
If you don't pull me out!'

'My beard is black,
There's soot in my sack,
My nose is tickling too!'

When Santa got stuck up the chimney,
'Aaachoo, achoo, achoo!'"

TRADITIONAL

ଯ

It was a moment any parent would like to bottle and keep forever. The little ones were having a ball. When Santa was laying down the requirements necessary to ensure the toys were delivered, they pointed their right forefinger at the audience, with the left hand on their hip. They were talking about their hero, the man of the moment, and the Christmas countdown was on – such excitement, such joy and such innocence.

That innocence was also very obvious in a tradition that Gay Byrne maintained every Christmas season on his radio show. Each year, without fail, he'd read 'Yes Virginia', the editorial published in the *New York Sun* in 1897. Eight-year-old Virginia O'Hanlon wrote to the editor wanting to know if Santa existed because some of her friends were saying there was no such person. It's a beautiful piece of writing.

ॐ

"Yes Virginia, there is a Santa Claus. He exists as certainly as love and generosity exist, and you know that they abound and give your life its highest beauty and joy."

NEW YORK SUN

ॐ

I have to say that Gay Byrne performed it beautifully too. It's a lovely celebration of the magic and joy of Christmas.

ॐ

"No Santa Claus! Thank God! He lives, and he lives forever. A thousand years from now, Virginia, nay, ten times ten thousand years from now, he will continue to make glad the heart of childhood."

NEW YORK SUN

Less innocent, but nonetheless traditional, was Gay's rendition of making the Christmas cake. You know the one where he'd read out the ingredients and pretend he was having a drop of the whiskey all the while he was making the cake. He'd end up stocious and slurring his words and the cake would end up all over the place. It was such a funny recitation and he is such a good performer. I can remember one Christmas listening to it in the car and the tears were rolling down my face. I could hardly see!

Listening to Gay Byrne in the run up to Christmas was something we all looked forward to and of course to his programme from Grafton Street on Christmas Eve. I never went into town for the show. The children were too small and too excited at the prospect of the night's happenings but I listened to it avidly.

When my children were still small some new Christmas songs were penned. They've stood the test of time and have become classic seasonal favourites. Wham's 'Last Christmas' is a good example. It was released in 1984, the year Eva, my eldest daughter was born.

৵

"Last Christmas, I gave you my heart
But the very next day, You gave it away
This year, to save me from tears
I'll give it to someone special."

GEORGE MICHAEL

That's still a must in our house every year. It's also a must to pronounce 'gave' the way Wham did; I 'gev' you my heart; you 'gev' it away!

There was another Christmas song released that year which has a special place in my heart for a couple of reasons. 'Do They Know It's Christmas' was written by Bob Geldof and Midge Ure after Bob saw Michael Buerk's BBC report alerting the world to the fact that people were dying of famine in Ethiopia. Eva was ten months old at the time and I watched that same report with her on my knee. I was shocked by the images of emaciated listless babies, too weak to cry. I had a baby of my own and I imagined her in that situation. I could see her face on that screen. It was heart-breaking to watch. Nobody, adult or child, should have to suffer for lack of food and water. When I heard that Bob Geldof's reaction was to write this song to raise funds for Ethiopia I was so impressed. That he used his not inconsiderable powers of persuasion to gather together a group of big stars to be a part of Band Aid was equally impressive – singers like Phil Collins, Paul Young, Bono, George Michael, Sade, and of course Boy George whose vocals on the piece are hauntingly beautiful.

"There's a world outside your window
And it's a world of dread and fear
Where the only water flowing is the bitter sting of tears
And the Christmas bells that ring there
Are the clanging chimes of doom
Well tonight thank God it's them instead of you."

BOB GELDOF/MIDGE URE

ॐ

I was very moved by that song. I've been to Ethiopia since and to other countries in Africa and seen first hand the struggle the people have to eke out a living "underneath that burning sun".

There are periods of drought and awful suffering still.

ॐ

"Where nothing ever grows, no rain or rivers flow..."

BOB GELDOF/MIDGE URE

ॐ

Thank goodness for people like Bob Geldof and Band Aid, who not only raise money to alleviate that suffering, but who also raise awareness of our responsibility to look to the needs of those less well off, particularly at Christmas time, the season of love and goodwill.

ॐ

"And in our world of plenty we can spread a smile of joy
Throw your arms around the world at Christmas time."

BOB GELDOF/MIDGE URE

Another modern classic is 'Fairytale of New York', from 1988. What an amazing piece of writing, the melody and the lyrics. It's full of anger, love, hate, regret, but above all, passion. I find the last lines very poignant.

ॐ

"I could have been someone
Well so could anyone
You took my dreams from me
When I first found you
I kept them with me babe
I put them with my own
Can't make it on my own
I've built my dreams around you."

SHANE MACGOWAN/JEM FINER

ॐ

The passion is spent. It's replaced by something gentle, sad, with regret for what might have been. Well done Shane McGowan and Jem Finer. And well done Shane and the late Kirsty MacColl for such a soulful performance. That's another must in our house at Christmas. It makes me think of the people who don't like Christmas. Maybe they're alone; maybe they've suffered loss. 'Fairytale' is many people's story.

Christmas is a special time – a time for giving, for thinking of others and for remembering absent friends. In Poland, an extra place is set at the Christmas table for that reason and also to symbolise a welcome for the passing stranger, maybe somebody who's got nowhere else to go, a 'Fairytale of New York' type of person. I like that custom, that spirit at Christmas time. It reminds me of our custom of putting the candle in the window. These lines from The Wexford Carol give an insight into that meaning of the Christmas message.

ॐ

"Good people all, this Christmas time,
Consider well and bear in mind
What our good God for us has done
In sending his beloved Son."

TWELFTH CENTURY TRADITIONAL IRISH

ॐ

Wouldn't it be nice if we all opened our hearts at Christmas time and allowed in the unconditional love and the joy that children feel?

It all helps to keep alive the magic of Christmas.

ॐ

"He sprang to his sleigh, to his team gave a whistle,
And away they all flew like the down of a thistle.
But I heard him exclaim, 'ere he drove out of sight,
'Happy Christmas to all, and to all a good night!'"

CLEMENT C MOORE